SELECTIONS FROM THE BRONTËS

SELECTIONS FROM
THE BRONTËS

Being Extracts from the Novels of
Charlotte and Emily Brontë

EDITED BY

H. A. TREBLE

CAMBRIDGE
AT THE UNIVERSITY PRESS
1927

CAMBRIDGE
UNIVERSITY PRESS

University Printing House, Cambridge CB2 8BS, United Kingdom

Published in the United States of America by Cambridge University Press, New York

Cambridge University Press is part of the University of Cambridge.

It furthers the University's mission by disseminating knowledge in the pursuit of
education, learning and research at the highest international levels of excellence.

www.cambridge.org
Information on this title: www.cambridge.org/9781107689602

© Cambridge University Press 1927

First published 1927
First paperback edition 2014

A catalogue record for this publication is available from the British Library

ISBN 978-1-107-68960-2 Paperback

PREFACE

THE reaction of modern times against what is usually called Victorianism—a reaction affecting such different writers as Dickens, Tennyson, and Browning—has led to general neglect of the once famous Brontë sisters and their work. *Jane Eyre*, *Wuthering Heights* and *Villette* are regarded nowadays as a somewhat overwrought and eccentric articulation of woman's earliest struggle for freedom from the bonds of mid-nineteenth-century convention. The masculine and half-sinister atmosphere, which even to us in these days of an almost complete emancipation seems to cling to their work, has helped to keep alive an early prejudice that placed *Jane Eyre* on a kind of Index Expurgatorius and condemned the work of Emily and Charlotte as an outburst of unwomanly passion. Time and changing custom have only emphasized the present neglect. True, the perverse criticism of to-day, habitually mistaking crudity for originality and eccentricity for genius in ancient and modern alike, has hailed *Wuthering Heights* as a psychological *tour de force*; but even that unique novel gathers dust on the book-shelf; it is a past and outworn triumph. While Jane Austen has been exalted—and rightly exalted—in modern critical judgment, the Brontës and George Eliot have for the most part had to give way before the more ephemeral smartness of women writers of to-day.

Little apology, therefore, is needed for a book of extracts which have been chosen to represent the best elements in the work of Charlotte and Emily Brontë. The nature description, so finely reminiscent of the atmosphere of their bleak moorland home, the characterization, and the peculiar autobiographical interest which literary magazines have unnecessarily exploited during the past few years, have their place in this selection. It may indeed be claimed that the passages printed here are part of the best literature of the last century.

The Introduction owes, of necessity, much to Mrs Gaskell's *Life* and to the late Clement Shorter's work on the Brontës.

H. A. TREBLE

CROYDON
May 1927

CONTENTS

INTRODUCTION

I T is very difficult to approach, and almost impossible to interpret, the work of the Brontë sisters except by way of their life. Mrs Gaskell and, in our own time, the late Mr Clement Shorter have revealed to us as much as we need to know of their inner life and character. The parish register, with its familiarly laconic entries, fixes for us the land where they dwelt in body and, for the most part, in spirit:

Baptisms solemnized in the parish of Bradford and Chapelry of Thornton in the County of York[1]

When baptized	Child's Christian Name	Parents' Names		Abode	Quality, Trade or Profession	By whom the Ceremony was Performed
		Christian	Sur-Name			
1816 29th June	Charlotte daughter of	The Rev. Patrick and Maria	Brontë	Thorn-ton	Minister of Thorn-ton	Wm. Morgan Minister of Christ Church Bradford
1817 July 23	Patrick Branwell son of	Patrick and Maria	Brontë	Thorn-ton	Minister	Jno. Fennell officiating Minister
1818 20th August	Emily Jane daughter of	The Rev. Patrick and Maria	Brontë A.B.	Thorn-ton Parson-age	Minister of Thorn-ton	Wm. Morgan Minister of Christ Church Bradford
1820 March 25th	Anne daughter of	The Rev. Patrick and Maria	Brontë	Minister of Haworth		Wm. Morgan Minister of Christchurch Bradford

[1] Taken from Clement Shorter's *The Brontës and their Circle*.

It also reminds us of their descent from Patrick Brontë, "Minister of Thornton," a stern parish priest whom later investigation has taught us to admire rather than despise. Thus it records those two elemental facts, of countryside and home, which reveal themselves so clearly in the life and work of the daughters. Their Yorkshire was a land remote, bleak, unfriendly; and their spiritual outlook inherited something of its wild loneliness. Home, with its stern and religious discipline, threw them back on an introspective imagination that throve well on the rude romance of their surroundings. Perhaps, even, some slight Celtic strain in their father's blood bequeathed to his children that weirdness and belief in "fey" which characterizes all the novels. Even young Branwell, who caused father and sisters so much pain, had a portion of the heritage, which he but wasted, like a prodigal, with riotous living.

The three sisters were born between the years 1816 and 1820 at Thornton in Yorkshire, and Charlotte, the first-born of the three, was the last of them to die, in 1855. Emily was just thirty when she died, and Anne only twenty-nine. The life of Anne makes the simplest and shortest chronicle. She lived it all, with a gentle charm and grace foreign to her sisters, within the bounds of her native county. Only two positions as governess—both faithfully described in *Agnes Grey*—punctuated her short life. *Agnes Grey* breathes a little of her gentleness; *The Tenant of Wildfell Hall* is merely her futile attempt to emulate the grim romance of *Wuthering Heights*. Her pathetic little poem

> I hop'd that with the brave and strong
> My portion'd task should lie

stands in similar contrast to Emily's defiant

> No coward soul is mine.

It may be, too, that Charlotte, portraying the virility and strength of Emily in Shirley Keeldar, described in

Catherine Helstone her youngest sister's gentleness. We cannot but be glad, however, that Anne's name, which would else have been forgotten, has survived in the brighter glory of her sisters'.

The lives of Charlotte and Emily were more eventful. Up to Emily's death in 1848 they may be taken as one, though, except for the actual periods at the Haworth home and a brief nine months in Brussels, they were not lived together. But the chief experiences of life were common to the two sisters. They may be summed up briefly thus:

1. Early years at home at Haworth [1816–24].
2. School Life—
    (a) at Cowan Bridge (the "Lowood" of *Jane Eyre*) [1824–25].
    (b) at Roe Head: Charlotte, 1831–2; Emily, 1835.
3. Governess Life in England [1837–40]:
    Charlotte at Stonegappe and Harrogate; Emily for a few months at Halifax.
4. Life at the Pensionnat Héger, Brussels:
    Charlotte, 1842, 1843–44; Emily, 1842.
5. Later Days at Haworth [1844–48]:
    Visit of Charlotte and Emily to London, July 1848; death of Branwell, September 1848; death of Emily, December 1848.

To this brief summary, which is adequate to the outward life of Emily, must be added those experiences that made Charlotte's life fuller and richer than that of her sisters. An inexplicable charm drew to her, quite early in life, two lovers; the later years brought two more. The first two were curates, and the faint memory of them is perhaps enshrined in the curates of *Shirley*. One of the later lovers was an official in the firm of her publishers, and the other was the Rev. Arthur Nicholls, her father's curate, to whom she was eventually married. Recent years have brought to light a possible love-story which exceeded all the others in fire and devotion. Charlotte herself has told the tale in *Villette*—as the passionate love of Lucy Snowe for M. Paul Emanuel. It is said that during her second visit to Brussels in 1843 Charlotte *lived* the story which she has depicted with such power and desperate reality; that, in fact, Lucy Snowe was Charlotte Brontë and Paul Emanuel was M. Héger, the Professor of the Pensionnat. The facts matter but little here and, except as they shed a new light on *Villette*, are better left alone.

The later years, that brought her a husband, gave her also a distinguished friend. Thackeray had read and admired *Jane Eyre*, and in her visits to London in 1850 and 1851 its author benefited by his personal friendship. Nevertheless these later years had their sorrow, for the prodigality of Branwell and the death of her two sisters had left Charlotte very much alone. *Shirley*, which was published in the year after Emily's death, betrays a sadness and gloom prevailing in spite of a growing fame and prosperity.

Out of the brief and restricted life of Emily have emerged a few poems, notable for their fierce strength, and one novel, *Wuthering Heights*. That book is unique in English. Its importance and intrinsic worth have been variously estimated, simply because it is possible to regard it in two totally different ways. Let it be considered an *objective* book, one of the many attempts at romantic tragedy in English, and in spite of, or even because of, its crude strength, it remains a violent, hectic failure. But if it is thought of as a *subjective* book, a revelation of the soul of Emily, it may take the place which some critics have given it among the greatest works of women writers. And, after all, the subjective interpretation is probably the truer. It was Matthew Arnold who wrote of the "passion, vehemence, grief, daring" of this woman's soul[1], and no less a person than Charlotte who

[1] *Haworth Churchyard, April* 1855.

pictured it in the life of Shirley Keeldar. The fierce, proud mental courage and physical rigour that fashioned the grim tale of Heathcliff and Earnshaw was characteristic of the woman who could sear the mad dog's bite with a hot iron. That incident, true of Emily and recorded of Shirley, affords some insight into the heart of both Charlotte and her sister; and we are left to postulate a subjective rather than an objective *Wuthering Heights*— a tale beaten, crudely enough maybe, out of the spiritual experience of her brief life.

In treating of Charlotte and her work we are on surer ground. The essence of her best and highest writing is autobiographical. Her life, which had three main periods, is recorded faithfully in her three chief novels. The greatness of *Jane Eyre* and *Villette* lies in that frank spiritual revelation of their writer; and if *Shirley* is less revealing, it is only because in that book Charlotte tried to be more objective in theme and character, and to picture her own life, as in a glass darkly, through the life of her sister. The other lesser novel, *The Professor*, which had to wait for a publisher, has a charm of its own as a miniature of what was to become a full picture in *Villette*.

That self-interpretation which we have seen to be the key-note of the work of all the sisters is evident in both the general treatment and the detail of the novels. It is interesting to look at the natural background and see therein the spiritual atmosphere of the revelation. Even Anne faintly pictures the cold and rainy gloom of her setting; but the passive Nature in her writings develops, with Charlotte, into animate being, throbbing with the writer's own heart, like the storm in *Lear*; and with Emily into a cruel, malignant, but impersonal thing that, in the remarkable opening chapters of *Wuthering Heights*, makes even the snow seem dark and sinister. But beyond that half-Shakespearean "first scene," there is in Emily's book but little deliberate nature-description—only that bleak background to the tragedy of the Heathcliffs, Earnshaws, and Lintons.

Charlotte differs from Emily in the degree of her power for nature-description, and partly in her attitude. To her, Nature was a more intimate thing, a sharer in human passions; there is about her work (as, indeed, there is about the work of such great artists as Shakespeare and Mr Hardy) a continual belief in, and exposition of, what has been called "the pathetic fallacy." But she had, too, in the descriptions themselves, the keen eye and sure hand of the artist. Various critics have praised that superb sense of colour and form which she betrays, half casually, in the description of the pictures which Jane Eyre showed to Mr Rochester:

These pictures were in water-colours. The first represented clouds, low and livid, rolling over a swollen sea: all the distance was in eclipse; so, too, was the foreground; or rather the nearest billows, for there was no land. One gleam of light lifted into relief a half-submerged mast, on which sat a cormorant, dark and large, with wings flecked with foam....

It is worth noticing that that same love of pictures and their descriptions is reproduced also in both *Villette* and *Shirley*. Her eye—the artist's eye—made a faithful portrayal, even if the heart often lifted Nature up into imagination and passion. The tints were generally sombre and the landscape desolate. There is but little of spring and summer in any of the novels, and if by chance a warm June or July day creeps in, there is usually, far off or near, the threatening of thunder. Yet Charlotte can be tranquil with the beautiful sadness of winter. After the pain and sordidness of Lowood, with the kindly Mrs Fairfax and Thornfield Hall promising better things, she is in such a mood of tranquillity; and that second maturer part of Jane Eyre's life begins with what is nothing less than a January idyll:

It was three o'clock; the church bell tolled as I passed under the belfry: the charm of the hour lay in its approaching dim-

ness, in the low-gliding and pale-beaming sun. I was a mile
from Thornfield, in a lane noted for wild-roses in summer, for
nuts and blackberries in autumn, and even now possessing
a few coral treasures in hips and haws, but whose best winter
delight lay in its utter solitude and leafless repose. If a breath
of air stirred, it made no sound here; for there was not a holly,
not an evergreen to rustle, and the stripped hawthorn and hazel
bushes were as still as the white, worn stones which causewayed
the middle of the path. Far and wide, on each side, there were
only fields, where no cattle now browsed; and the little brown
birds, which stirred occasionally in the hedge, looked like single
russet leaves that had forgotten to drop.

But the winds soon begin to ride through *Jane Eyre*. On
the night before that broken wedding, the gale blows
about the house, in wild and fearful harmony with Jane's
dream. Even when she returns, long afterwards, to the
blind and ageing Rochester at Ferndean, it was "just ere
dark on an evening marked by the characteristics of sad
sky, cold gale, and continued small penetrating rain."

In *Villette* the relief of a brighter Nature is withheld
just as sternly and deliberately, except, perhaps, on the
one occasion of Madame Beck's fête, when the sun did
shine for a whole day while Lucy Snowe, ironically
enough, sat imprisoned in the attic learning her part at
the command of the excited and irate Paul Emanuel.
Autumn is even more pitiless than it is in *Jane Eyre*.
During that long vacation at the Pensionn̄at when
October draws in, the raging storm and beating rain
crush Lucy with a deadly paralysis. The tempest tosses
her as a leaf and she is broken in its desolation. It is
winter-time, with snow, while she dwells in the comfort
of Mrs Bretton's love and Graham's stately kindness;
but there is a "November drizzle" on the night when
she returns to Madame Beck's. After that the atmosphere
in *Villette* is electrically charged, like Paul Emanuel's
mind and heart. There are few better things in the novels
than that description of the thunderstorm which broke

over Villette when Lucy had called at the house of Madame Walravens and Père Silas, and had heard the ancient love of her professor (see pp. 42–5). But the electric air is apparent often, both in and out of doors. It makes Lucy tremble a little when she is hiding her letters in the pear-tree from the prying eyes of Madame Beck and Monsieur Paul:

> The air of the night was very still, but dim with a peculiar mist, which changed the moonlight into a luminous haze. In this air, or this mist, there was some quality—electrical, perhaps—which acted in strange sort upon me. I felt then as I had felt a year ago in England—on a night when the aurora borealis was streaming and sweeping round heaven, when, belated in lonely fields, I had paused to watch that mustering of an army with banners—that quivering of serried lances— that swift ascent of messengers from below the north star to the dark, high keystone of heaven's arch.

There is Charlotte the artist again, painting this time a picture of wild flaming colour.

In *Shirley* Nature, like everything else, is more objective, less "personal." *Shirley* is, indeed, the most Yorkshire of all the novels, and its Nature is of the land rather than of the atmosphere. Hollow's Cottage, Briarmains, and "the extensive and solitary sweep of Nunnely Common" make a lone physical background, suggesting, however faintly, that mute, strong "presence" with which a later novelist was to endue Egdon Heath. Here, too, is that queer sense of irony which has been noted already in connection with Madame Beck's fête: it is a beautiful summer night when Moore's mill is attacked, and Shirley and Caroline Helstone watch the human tumult against the calm of starlit sky. But their unquiet, restless loves move with slow and troublous progress against the cold background of the countryside. The book is full of neutral tones, having but little of that vital description which characterizes *Jane Eyre*, and especially *Villette*. But here and there Nature becomes suggestively sad, as if it were in a ballad. Thus, when Moore and Yorke are immersed in their confessional of love and life at Rushedge, Yorke turns suddenly:

"The moon is up," was his first not quite relevant remark, pointing with his whip across the moor. "There she is, rising into the haze, staring at us wi' a strange red glower. She is no more silver than old Helstone's brow is ivory. What does she mean by leaning her cheek on Rushedge i' that way, and looking at us wi' a scowl and a menace?"

And over the subsequent scene of the attempted murder of Moore the same moon shines calmly, reflecting her blood-red light:

"What now?" Moore said, addressing his horse, which, hearing the ripple of water, and feeling thirsty, turned to a wayside trough, where the moonbeam was playing in a crystal eddy.
"Yorke," pursued Moore, "ride on: I must let him drink."
....A fierce flash and sharp crack violated the calm of night. Yorke, ere he turned, knew the four convicts of Birmingham were avenged.

It would not be unfair to either book to compare the Nature depicted in *Shirley* with that in *Wuthering Heights*: the crude strength of Emily balancing the finer artistry of Charlotte in framing the lone Yorkshire background for the story.

The treatment of Nature in the novels cannot be left without some reference to that suggestion of the supernatural which pervades the books. We are early introduced to it in *Wuthering Heights* in the cold white hand of Catherine Linton at the window, stretched out of the midnight snow. It rings through *Jane Eyre* in the wild, mysterious shriek of Rochester's mad wife; and it is conjured up less fearfully by that queer but powerful scene where Rochester, disguised as an old fortune-teller, drawls out to Jane Eyre astoundingly true words about her life and heart. In *Villette* it appears as the nun who steps conveniently out of the legend of the garden to frighten poor Lucy Snowe when she ascends to the attic, or walks quietly in the *allée défendue*. *Shirley*, perhaps, lacks it, unless we feel a supernatural foreboding all through the book, born of the whispering anger that surrounds Moore, the real centre of the story.

But this feature, wherever and however it comes, is part of something deeper in the nature of Emily and Charlotte. To the two sisters romance seemed to spell the ugly, the sinister, even the grim. The "supernatural solicitings" are but the outward reflection of the romantic presentiment of an overshadowing evil. There is a queer, and perhaps accidental, illustration of this in three of the novels, *Wuthering Heights*, *Jane Eyre*, and *Shirley*, in each of which so homely and familiar a thing as a dog seems to appear with some foreboding of disaster to come. It appears, even more clearly, in some of the characters themselves—Heathcliff's brutality, Rochester's ugliness, Mrs Yorke's angularity, Madame Beck's silent steps and spying eyes. Some of this dark romance is the result of a lack of humour. The bleak greyness of the novels becomes, in itself, unnatural, unrelieved as it is by the sunshine with which a Shakespeare and a Hardy would both brighten and intensify their tragedy.

That "masculinity" of thought which had its outward expression in the assumed names of the sisters—Currer, Ellis, and Acton Bell—was apparent particularly in their characterization. Their portrayal of Nature is unfeminine, of human nature, less feminine still. Emily hardly draws characters at all. She personifies hatred and bitterness, fierceness and revenge; hews her Heathcliff and Earnshaw out of stone, violently and crudely, but leaves them with a certain terrible strength. Charlotte, artist as she was, had nothing of the skill for delicate miniature which so characterized Jane Austen. The two greatest characters of her novels are but two pictures of the same living woman, and that woman Charlotte Brontë herself. Here we have the essence of what has

been called her "spiritual biography." It is interesting
to trace in the characters of Jane Eyre and Lucy Snowe
those essential qualities of mind and heart that belonged
to the writer herself; to set the other men and women of
the novels in the light of the two governesses who served
faithfully at Thornfield and at the Rue Fossette, but had
so strong and passionate a soul behind the patient service.
Plain, simply dressed, governess in the house of Rochester,
teacher of English in the school of Madame Beck—that
is the background for the workings of the heart. So parson
Brontë's daughter lived unassuming, sturdily independent, decided in love and hatred, at school and home,
as governess in England and at the Pensionnat des Dames.
The outward and the inward flame she has portrayed in
two different degrees and in two different scenes. There
is an almost dogged steadiness, broken by grief and pain
after the dramatic wedding scene, in Jane Eyre's love
for Rochester. But the dour Northern passion becomes
a fierce burning flame in Lucy Snowe's love for Paul
Emanuel. The two descriptions build up the one character.

But if the novelist could picture herself with truth and
vigour, she had some difficulty with the characters which
she grouped around her. In the main, it is true, they are
from life; but they are often curiously warped and even
unjustly drawn. Perhaps it is natural for a woman to
falter in portraying another woman. Even the minor
characters, like Mrs Reed in *Jane Eyre*, Ginevra Fanshawe and Zélie St Pierre in *Villette*, Hortense Moore
and Mrs Yorke in *Shirley*, are overdrawn by that rather
bitter prejudice which seemed to possess Charlotte—the
same prejudice that made a Lowood out of the merely
gloomy and colourless Cowan Bridge. The truth is that
Charlotte, like most "strong" women, was as deficient
in real sympathy as in humour. When she tries to be
tender, she is merely patronizing, as in the picture of
Caroline Helstone. With her, quiet force could cover
a multitude of sins. There is more than a trace of admira-

tion in Lucy Snowe for Madame Beck. All the cat-like, spying methods of Madame seem to be condoned for the sake of that iron strength with which she ruled everybody, from her kinsman Paul down to "*la portresse*." And that admiration, characteristic of Jane Eyre and Lucy Snowe alike, is reflected objectively in the picture of Shirley. Shirley is Charlotte's symbol of womanhood; a description of Emily; but more than that—a personification of that masculinity which is typical of both sisters. Caroline Helstone is the Victorian woman, working her sampler, pining for love, wondering at Miss Keeldar, her friend. But that friend knows no convention. To be "Shirley Keeldar, Esq." is a fond yet serious imagination of her mind. She bursts those bonds which fettered other women to a tradition of sweet, inactive simplicity. With one swift tumultuous torrent she overwhelms the amazed Mr Sympson—personification of that foolish masculine authority which could no more curb the woman's will than a few rioters could stop the onward progress of Moore's machines. She flings Donne into the street for presuming upon the mere fact that he was a man. Even Moore is humbled to the dust by the woman whom he thought to honour by what she deemed his paltry love. Jane Eyre, Lucy Snowe, Shirley Keeldar are true characters; but they are also the mouthpiece of that woman's longing for emancipation which had its fulfil- ment about eighty years afterwards, in our own times.

"Author's heroines," says Caroline Helstone, "are almost as good as an authoress's heroes." "Not at all," says Shirley; "women read men more truly than men read women."

That is a piece of Charlotte's self-revelation, both as novelist and as woman. She had a certain pride in reading men's hearts, and a sure confidence in her diagnosis. Her father's latest curate and M. Héger of Brussels afforded her equal practice in her peculiar art. There is a special interest, therefore, in the men of the novels. Three stand out particularly—Mr Rochester, M. Paul Emanuel, and Gérard Moore. They make a strange trio; and the woman who portrays them reveals in herself a queer love of that mingled gloom and passion which marks her heroes. Rochester is ugly of frame and darkly passionate of heart; Paul Emanuel is well-nigh laughable in the violence of his hate and love; Gérard Moore is as grim and rigid as one of his own machines, and as unhuman, till the combined force of Shirley and a bullet humanizes him for the love of Caroline Helstone. It was doubtless her own strong will and masculine independence that caused her to depict men thus. She admires in men (and perhaps in women) a mental strength that is apt to verge on brutality. Physical strength does not satisfy her; Malone in *Shirley* is dismissed, for all his muscle, as lightly as the little effeminate Sweeting. It is curious to observe how even the secondary characters have some share of that mental resolution she admires so much. The ending of *Jane Eyre* is almost lyric with the asceticism of St John Rivers:

He entered on the path he had marked for himself; he pursues it still. A more resolute, indefatigable pioneer never wrought amidst rocks and dangers. Firm, faithful, and devoted, . . . he labours for his race; he clears their painful way to improvement; he hews down like a giant the prejudices of creed and caste that encumber it. He may be stern; he may be exacting; he may be ambitious yet; but his is the sternness of the warrior Greatheart, who guards his pilgrim convoy from the onslaught of Apollyon.

But, for all this, he has not the passion to satisfy Jane Eyre's love; for that she has to return to Rochester of the scarred face and blinded eyes. So, in the later novel, Graham Bretton, as boy and man, stalks up and down the pages as a kind of guardian angel to Lucy in loneliness, tempest, and fire. But his love rewards her with only a few casual letters, which she leaves mouldering in the old pear-tree when the fire of Emanuel has set her heart aflame. In *Shirley* the situation changes a little. For a while Jane Eyre and Lucy Snowe mislead us and themselves as to their true lovers; but this misleading amounts, in Shirley, to a dramatic perversity. It is an unexpected *dénouement* when Shirley's strength of mind is conferred on Louis Moore's aesthetic sentiment, and Caroline's gentleness on Gérard's proud imperious will.

But of all Charlotte's men Paul Emanuel is the most interesting because he is the most human. Both Rochester and Moore have something of the monster about them; but if we dig deep beneath the wayward eccentricity we find a man in M. Paul. For once, with the "austere regard," the burning passion, there is evident, if only fitfully, a touch of tenderness in Lucy's passion for her professor. *Villette* is, after all, the greatest evidence for the conjectured Héger love-story. Lucy Snowe's love is a matter of Charlotte Brontë's heart rather than a figment of her imagination. It is no wonder, then, that Emanuel is drawn with an intensity of truth, a vividness born of the experience of a woman naturally passionate and strong in mind and spirit. True, the exaggeration is so great as sometimes to become ludicrous. Paul moves and speaks like a fury. He raves in the class-room, storms up and down the garden and in the hall, shouts his invectives against England and Englishwomen when Lucy brings him nothing at his birthday fête. But where Rochester and even Moore are coldly sinister figures, Emanuel is moved by an excitable, childlike humanity, which makes us love him as we should love a wayward boy. His excesses are too often the strong petulant reaction to the lofty independence of "Mademoiselle Lucie" for us to give him anything but sympathy. And here and there the simple *naïveté* has in it a streak of gentleness which Charlotte portrays in no other character, not even in herself as Jane Eyre or Lucy Snowe.

The minor characters need but little comment. They are also, for the main part, actual pictures. It is interesting to notice, in the three chief novels, how Charlotte's firm will and independent mind fall back, now and then, upon a comfortable, familiar homeliness—as if she would rest a little from the outward turmoil and stress. So Jane Eyre warms to Mrs Fairfax as she sits, quietly reminiscent, the cat on her knee; Lucy Snowe is happy and content with Mrs Bretton to wait upon her during the days of nervous prostration; Caroline Helstone braves the valley of the shadow of death in the soft, but unknown, mother-love of Mrs Pryor. That escape from the passionate is particularly apparent in *Shirley*. Here Mr Yorke, Mr Hall, and even old Helstone (the somewhat unjust picture of Patrick Brontë) at once tone down and throw into relief the wilder elements in the tale. We are again reminded of the later novelist, who, in a grander and more skilful way, set the dark passions of Troy and Boldwood against the steady calm of Gabriel Oak.

The reference to Mr Hardy leads on naturally to a comparison and a contrast. He shares with Charlotte and Emily Brontë a love of melodrama. It is as dominant in *Far from the Madding Crowd* or *The Mayor of Casterbridge* as it is in *Jane Eyre*. It becomes a defect, an offence against art, in his work as well as in that of the Brontës. But it is also as natural to him as to them. He is of the West, they of the North; he depicts, in scenes made sometimes unnaturally vivid, the poignancy of sorrow; they, in similar scenes, depict its crude, bare hardness. His heritage is of Wessex, theirs of Yorkshire. There is a geographical difference of attitude to grief and tragedy. Yet that is not all. Mr Hardy had a supreme gift which neither Charlotte nor Emily Brontë ever had. A careful reading of all the Brontë novels will not discover a solitary gleam of true humour. There is a wry turn of language sometimes, especially in Charlotte, a kind of intellectual smile—no more. But Mr Hardy has the heart-felt elemental humour of Shakespeare; he re-creates and revivifies the spirit of Peter Quince, Bully

Bottom, and Autolycus. In the Brontës not only is there little gentleness; there is no laughter of the heart.

It is profitable, too, to compare the work of the sisters with that of two other women novelists of their century—Jane Austen and George Eliot. Jane Austen painted upon a tiny canvas; her work was exquisite in its detail. She had a wonderful sensitiveness to little things. Life, as she knew it, lay within the confines of an English village. Above all, she watched and depicted the humour and irony of that world which she had made her own. Charlotte Brontë, painting with fiercer strokes on a wider mental canvas, lacked completely that exquisiteness of touch and thought which has secured for Jane Austen the highest place among women novelists. Now and then in *Shirley* there is the attempt at satire—in the curates and the Sympsons; but we are left sighing for Mr Collins and Mrs Bennett. It seems strange that the woman who in the preface to *Jane Eyre* expressed so great an admiration for the satire and humour of Thackeray should herself be devoid of both. But the remark of Scott about her littleness of interests while England was shaken by the Napoleonic wars throws light upon Jane Austen's genius. Her littleness was, after all, the essence of greatness. Charlotte Brontë is the lesser novelist because she had no eye for those fine points which make the comedy or tragedy of character. In her girlhood days she, like Shirley, had turned her eyes away from the men about her to give an odd, pompous love to "Arthur Wellesley, Duke of Wellington." She could see only the broad outlines of character, as if she surveyed it from afar.

George Eliot stands, perhaps, a little nearer to the Brontës. She has humour, it is true; and her novels have a softer, a southern aspect that contrasts strongly with the cold moorland atmosphere of *Jane Eyre* and *Wuthering Heights*. Her humour itself gives her more pathos, more humanity. Nowhere among the Brontë characters is there a Hetty Sorrel, or a Maggie Tulliver, or such an

idyll as Silas Marner's love for Effie. Yet there are traces,
even outside her deliberate "preaching," of that sense
of tragic evil and brooding sorrow that marks Charlotte's
work; and a hint of that austerity with which both Emily
and Charlotte faced life and destiny.

The style of the Brontës needs but little comment.
Wuthering Heights is as crude in its language as it is in
theme. There are in it the petulant strokes of the painter
with an eye for colour, but none of the niceties of the
artist who cares for harmony and beauty of form. We
have noted that Charlotte had that very sense of artistry
which Emily lacked. The Nature passages already quoted
exemplify to the full her observance of Nature and her
skill in expression when she set out to describe what she
saw. In such descriptions, and, indeed, throughout her
books, she had a virility of style and an aversion from
the merely passive which give to some of the chapters
an unreal, exaggerated force. That love of "active"
language is reflected in her abundant use of French, not
only throughout *Villette*, but also here and there in *Jane
Eyre* and *Shirley*. It was a love which, having its origin
in her own passionate spirit, was naturally intensified
during her Continental sojourn. Hence we find that the
purely narrative parts of the novels move quickly. There
is a swift and sure description at the moment of climax
or crisis—Rochester and Jane Eyre at the altar, Paul
Emanuel's birthday, the fight at Hollow's Mill. Nevertheless, the three chief novels are long and slow in the
development of plot. They are full of what we should
call to-day psychological explanations, philosophic
deductions, presented usually in those confidential
"asides" and appeals to the reader which were so
beloved of Victorian writers. Thus the natural force of
language, at its strongest and best in the simple narrative,
too often spends itself in moral and philosophic argument.
George Eliot's habit of preaching, which spoils for us the
artistry of *Adam Bede* and *The Mill on the Floss*, forms an

obvious parallel to Charlotte's persistent commentary
on character and incident. It is, perhaps, interesting to
note how the stern Christianity of the Haworth days
often inspired Charlotte to enrich her dullest philosophies
with references to the grimmer stories and characters
of the Old Testament. But that love and knowledge of
the Bible were perhaps as natural to her as they have
been to every great prose-writer in English since 1611.

The Brontës are experiencing to-day that reaction of
criticism which has been the fate, in turn, of most of the
Victorian writers. George Eliot and even Thackeray
and Dickens have suffered eclipse with them. Only the
passing of years can bring the clear vision and the just
estimate, and we can feel that something at least of the
strange genius of Charlotte and Emily will remain for
the reckoning of posterity.

BIBLIOGRAPHICAL DETAILS

1. *Poems by Currer, Ellis and Acton Bell*. London, Aylott and Jones, 8 Paternoster Row, 1846. This was the title of the first published work of the sisters. The book was printed at their own expense, and only two copies were sold. Remainder copies were afterwards bound up by Messrs Smith and Elder. In modern times *The Professor* and the *Poems* are usually printed together in one volume (e.g. *The World's Classics* edition). Except for the intrinsic worth of one or two of Emily's poems, this collection is of interest only as the early work of genius that developed later in another direction.

2. *Jane Eyre* was sent to Messrs Smith and Elder on their courteous rejection of *The Professor* (probably as being too short for success in the days of the three-volume novel). The MS. was "read" by Mr W. S. Williams, the firm's official reader, was immediately accepted, and was published in October 1847. There was at once much speculation concerning the identity of the author, and many violent criticisms were hurled at its so-called "bad taste." These criticisms Charlotte answered in the Preface to the second edition, in which she also paid a tribute to the work of Thackeray.

3. *Wuthering Heights* by Ellis Bell and *Agnes Grey* by Acton Bell were published together as a three-volume novel by Thomas Newby in December 1847, three months after *Jane Eyre* had made the pseudonym of "Bell" famous.

4. *The Tenant of Wildfell Hall* by Acton Bell was published by Newby a year before Anne's death in 1848.

5. *Shirley* was submitted to Messrs Smith and Elder, the publishers of *Jane Eyre*. Much of the novel was written during the troublous year 1848, when both Branwell and Emily died and Anne began to sicken. Mr Clement Shorter prints one or two interesting letters of Charlotte to Mr Williams, the reader, concerning the novel, referring, e.g. to the question of title: shall it be *Hollow's Mill*, *Fieldhead*, or *Shirley*? It was published by Smith and Elder in 1849.

6. *Villette*, which represents the recasting of the original *The Professor*, was published by Messrs Smith and Elder in 1852.

7. *The Professor*, a Tale by Currer Bell, in two volumes. Smith Elder & Co., 65 Cornhill, 1857. Charlotte's rejected first novel was published two years after her death, with a note by her husband, the Rev. Arthur Nicholls.

8. Mrs Gaskell: *Life of Charlotte Brontë* (reprinted in *The World's Classics*), 1857.

9. *Charlotte Brontë and her Circle*. Clement Shorter. Hodder and Stoughton, 1896.

10. *Charlotte Brontë and her Sisters*. Clement Shorter. Hodder and Stoughton, 1905.

11. *The Brontës: Life and Letters*. Clement Shorter. Hodder and Stoughton, 1908.

12. *A Note on Charlotte Brontë*. A. C. Swinburne. Chatto and Windus, 1877.

13. *Life of Charlotte Brontë*. Augustine Birrell. Great Writers Series.

14. *Life of Emily J. Brontë*. Eminent Women Series.

15. *Charlotte Brontë*. 1816–1916. Centenary Memorial, 1918.

16. *The Brontë Family*. F. A. Leyland. 1886.

17. *In the Footsteps of the Brontës*. Mrs E. H. Chadwick. 1914.

18. *Brontë Moors and Villages*. Eliz. Southwart. John Lane, 1922.

19. *The Women Novelists*. R. B. Johnson. Collins, 1918.

20. *The Key to the Brontë Works*. J. Malham-Hembleby. Walter Scott, 1911.

THE ADVENTURE OF GOING ABROAD

from *Villette*.

M Y mistress being dead, and I once more alone, I had to look out for a new place. About this time I might be a little—a very little—shaken in nerves. I grant I was not looking well, but, on the contrary, thin, haggard, and hollow-eyed; like a sitter-up at night, like an over-wrought servant, or a placeless person in debt. In debt, however, I was not; nor quite poor; for though Miss Marchmont had not had time to benefit me, as, on that last night, she said she intended, yet, after the funeral, my wages were duly paid by her second cousin, the heir, an avaricious-looking man, with pinched nose and narrow temples, who, indeed, I heard long afterwards, turned out a thorough miser: a direct contrast to his generous kinswoman, and a foil to her memory, blessed to this day by the poor and needy. The possessor, then, of fifteen pounds; of health, though worn, not broken, and of a spirit in similar condition; I might still, in comparison with many people, be regarded as occupying an enviable position. An embarrassing one it was, however, at the same time; as I felt with some acuteness on a certain day, of which the corresponding one in the next week was to see my departure from my present abode, while with another I was not provided.

In this dilemma I went, as a last and sole resource, to see and consult an old servant of our family; once my nurse, now housekeeper at a grand mansion not far from Miss Marchmont's. I spent some hours with her; she comforted, but knew not how to advise me. Still all inward darkness, I left her about twilight; a walk of two miles lay before me; it was a clear, frosty night. In spite of my solitude, my poverty, and my perplexity my heart, nourished and nerved with the vigour of a youth that

had not yet counted twenty-three summers, beat light
and not feebly. Not feebly, I am sure, or I should have
trembled in that lonely walk, which lay through still
fields and passed neither village nor farmhouse, nor
cottage: I should have quailed in the absence of moonlight, for it was by the leading of stars only I traced the
dim path; I should have quailed still more in the un-
wonted presence of that which to-night shone in the
north, a moving mystery—the Aurora Borealis. But this
solemn stranger influenced me otherwise than through
my fears. Some new power it seemed to bring. I drew
in energy with the keen, low breeze that blew on its
path. A bold thought was sent to my mind; my mind
was made strong to receive it.

"Leave this wilderness," it was said to me, "and go
out hence."

"Where?" was the query.

I had not very far to look; gazing from this country
parish in that flat, rich middle of England—I mentally
saw within reach what I had never yet beheld with my
bodily eyes; I saw London.

The next day I returned to the hall, and asking once
more to see the housekeeper, I communicated to her my
plan.

Mrs Barrett was a grave, judicious woman, though she
knew little more of the world than myself; but grave and
judicious as she was, she did not charge me with being
out of my senses: and, indeed, I had a staid manner of
my own which ere now had been as good to me as cloak
and hood of hodden grey; since under its favour I had
been enabled to achieve with impunity, and even
approbation, deeds that, if attempted with an excited
and unsettled air, would in some minds have stamped
me as a dreamer and zealot.

The housekeeper was slowly propounding some
difficulties, while she prepared orange-rind for marmalade, when a child ran past the window and came

bounding into the room. It was a pretty child, and as it danced, laughing, up to me—for we were not strangers (nor, indeed, was its mother—a young married daughter of the house—a stranger)—I took it on my knee. Different as were our social positions now, this child's mother and I had been schoolfellows, when I was a girl of ten and she a young lady of sixteen; and I remembered her—good-looking, but dull—in a lower class than mine.

I was admiring the boy's handsome dark eyes, when the mother, young Mrs Leigh, entered. What a beautiful and kind-looking woman was the good-natured and comely, but unintellectual girl become! Wifehood and maternity had changed her thus, as I have since seen them change others even less promising than she. Me she had forgotten. I was changed too, though not, I fear, for the better. I made no attempt to recall myself to her memory; why should I? She came for her son to accompany her in a walk, and behind her followed a nurse, carrying an infant. I only mention the incident because, in addressing the nurse, Mrs Leigh spoke French (very bad French, by the way, and with an incorrigibly bad accent, again forcibly reminding me of our school-days): and I found the woman was a foreigner. The little boy chattered volubly in French too. When the whole party were withdrawn, Mrs Barrett remarked that her young lady had brought that foreign nurse home with her two years ago, on her return from a Continental excursion; that she was treated almost as well as a governess, and had nothing to do but walk out with the baby and chatter French with Master Charles; "and," added Mrs Barrett, "she says there are many Englishwomen in foreign families as well placed as she."

I stored up this piece of casual information, as careful housewives store seemingly worthless shreds and fragments for which their prescient minds anticipate a possible use some day. Before I left my old friend, she gave me the address of a respectable old-fashioned inn in the city, which, she said, my uncles used to frequent in former days.

In going to London, I ran less risk and evinced less enterprise than the reader may think. In fact, the distance was only fifty miles. My means would suffice both to take me there, to keep me a few days, and also to bring me back if I found no inducement to stay. I regarded it as a brief holiday, permitted for once to work-weary faculties, rather than as an adventure of life and death. There is nothing like taking all you do at a moderate estimate: it keeps mind and body tranquil; whereas grandiloquent notions are apt to hurry both into fever.

Fifty miles were then a day's journey (for I speak of a time gone by: my hair, which, till a late period, withstood the frosts of time, lies now, at last white, under a white cap, like snow beneath snow). About nine o'clock of a wet February night I reached London.

My reader, I know, is one who would not thank me for an elaborate reproduction of poetic first impressions; and it is well, inasmuch as I had neither time nor mood to cherish such: arriving as I did late, on a dark, raw, and rainy evening, in a Babylon and a wilderness, of which the vastness and the strangeness tried to the utmost any powers of clear thought and steady self-possession with which, in the absence of more brilliant faculties, Nature might have gifted me.

When I left the coach, the strange speech of the cab-men and others waiting round, seemed to me odd as a foreign tongue. I had never before heard the English language chopped up in that way. However, I managed to understand and to be understood, so far as to get myself and trunk safely conveyed to the old inn whereof I had the address. How difficult, how oppressive, how puzzling seemed my flight! In London for the first time; at an inn for the first time; tired with travelling; confused with darkness; palsied with cold; unfurnished with either experience or advice to tell me how to act, and yet—to act obliged.

Into the hands of common-sense I confided the matter. Common-sense, however, was as chilled and bewildered as all my other faculties, and it was only under the spur of an inexorable necessity that she spasmodically executed her trust. Thus urged, she paid the porter; considering the crisis, I did not blame her too much that she was hugely cheated; she asked the waiter for a room; she timorously called for the chambermaid; what is far more, she bore, without being wholly overcome, a highly supercilious style of demeanour from that young lady, when she appeared.

I recollect this same chambermaid was a pattern of town prettiness and smartness. So trim her waist, her cap, her dress—I wondered how they had all been manufactured. Her speech had an accent which in its mincing glibness seemed to rebuke mine as by authority; her spruce attire flaunted an easy scorn to my plain country garb.

"Well, it can't be helped," I thought, "and then the scene is new, and the circumstances; I shall gain good."

Maintaining a very quiet manner towards this arrogant little maid, and subsequently observing the same towards the parsonic-looking, black-coated, white-neck-clothed waiter, I got civility from them ere long. I believe at first they thought I was a servant; but in a little while they changed their minds, and hovered in a doubtful state between patronage and politeness.

I kept up well till I had partaken of some refreshment, warmed myself by a fire, and was fairly shut into my own room; but, as I sat down by the bed and rested my head and arms on the pillow, a terrible oppression overcame me. All at once my position rose on me like a ghost. Anomalous, desolate, almost blank of hope, it stood. What was I doing here alone in great London? What should I do on the morrow? What prospects had I in

life? What friends had I on earth? Whence did I come?
Whither should I go? What should I do?

I wet the pillow, my arms, and my hair, with rushing
tears. A dark interval of most bitter thought followed
this burst; but I did not regret the step taken, nor wish
to retract it. A strong, vague persuasion that it was
better to go forward than backward, and that I *could* go
forward—that a way, however narrow and difficult,
would in time open—predominated over other feelings:
its influence hushed them so far, that at last I became
sufficiently tranquil to be able to say my prayers and
seek my couch. I had just extinguished my candle and
lain down, when a deep, low, mighty tone swung through
the night. At first I knew it not; but it was uttered twelve
times, and at the twelfth colossal hum and trembling
knell, I said: "I lie in the shadow of St Paul's."

The next day was the first of March, and when I awoke,
rose and opened my curtain, I saw the risen sun struggling
through fog. Above my head, above the house-tops,
co-elevate almost with the clouds, I saw a solemn, orbed
mass, dark-blue and dim—THE DOME. While I looked,
my inner self moved: my spirit shook its always-fettered
wings half loose; I had a sudden feeling as if I, who never
yet truly lived, were at last about to taste life. In that
morning my soul grew as fast as Jonah's gourd.

"I did well to come," I said, proceeding to dress with
speed and care. "I like the spirit of this great London
which I feel around me. Who but a coward would pass
his whole life in hamlets, and for ever abandon his
faculties to the eating rust of obscurity?"

Being dressed, I went down; not travel-worn and
exhausted, but tidy and refreshed. When the waiter came
in with my breakfast, I managed to accost him sedately,
yet cheerfully; we had ten minutes' discourse, in the
course of which we became usefully known to each other.

He was a grey-haired elderly man; and, it seemed, had

lived in his present place twenty years. Having ascertained this, I was sure he must remember my two uncles, Charles and Wilmot, who, fifteen years ago, were frequent visitors here. I mentioned their names; he recalled them perfectly and with respect. Having intimated my connection, my position in his eyes was henceforth clear, and on a right footing. He said I was like my uncle Charles: I suppose he spoke truth, because Mrs Barrett was accustomed to say the same thing. A ready and obliging courtesy now replaced his former uncomfortably doubtful manner; henceforth I need no longer be at a loss for a civil answer to a sensible question.

The street on which my little sitting-room window looked was narrow, perfectly quiet, and not dirty: the few passengers were just such as one sees in provincial towns: here was nothing formidable; I felt sure I might venture out alone.

Having breakfasted, out I went. Elation and pleasure were in my heart: to walk alone in London seemed of itself an adventure. Presently I found myself in Paternoster Row—classic ground this. I entered a bookseller's shop, kept by one Jones: I bought a little book—a piece of extravagance I could ill afford; but I thought I would one day give or send it to Mrs Barrett. Mr Jones, a dried-in man of business, stood behind his desk: he seemed one of the greatest, and I one of the happiest of beings.

Prodigious was the amount of life I lived that morning. Finding myself before St Paul's, I went in; I mounted to the dome: I saw thence London, with its river, and its bridges, and its churches; I saw antique Westminster, and the green Temple Gardens, with sun upon them, and a glad, blue sky, of early spring above; and, between them and it, not too dense a cloud of haze.

Descending, I went wandering whither chance might lead, in a still ecstasy of freedom and enjoyment; and I got—I know not how—I got into the heart of city life.

I saw and felt London at last: I got into the Strand; I went up Cornhill; I mixed with the life passing along; I dared the perils of crossings. To do this, and to do it utterly alone, gave me, perhaps an irrational, but a real pleasure. Since those days I have seen the West End, the parks, the fine squares, but I love the city far better. The city seems so much more in earnest: its business, its rush, its roar, are such serious things, sights and sounds. The city is getting its living—the West End but enjoying its pleasure. At the West End you may be amused, but in the city you are deeply excited.

Faint, at last, and hungry (it was years since I had felt such healthy hunger), I returned, about two o'clock, to my dark, old and quiet inn. I dined on two dishes— a plain joint and vegetables; both seemed excellent: how much better than the small, dainty messes Miss March- mont's cook used to send up to my kind, dead mistress and me, and to the discussion of which we could not bring half an appetite between us! Delightfully tired, I lay down on three chairs for an hour (the room did not boast a sofa), I slept, then I woke and thought for two hours.

My state of mind, and all accompanying circumstances, were just now such as most to favour the adoption of a new, resolute and daring—perhaps desperate—line of action. I had nothing to lose. Unutterable loathing of a desolate existence past, forbade return. If I failed in what I now designed to undertake, who, save myself, would suffer? If I died far away from—home, I was going to say, but I had no home—from England, then, who would weep?

I might suffer; I was inured to suffering: death itself had not, I thought, those terrors for me which it has for the softly reared. I had, ere this, looked on the thought of death with a quiet eye. Prepared then for any con- sequences, I formed a project.

That same evening I obtained from my friend, the

waiter, information respecting the sailing of vessels for a certain continental port, Boue-Marine. No time, I found, was to be lost: that very night I must take my berth. I might, indeed, have waited till the morning before going on board, but would not run the risk of being too late.

"Better take your berth at once, ma'am," counselled the waiter. I agreed with him, and having discharged my bill, and acknowledged my friend's services at a rate which I now know was princely, and which in his eyes must have seemed absurd—and indeed, while pocketing the cash, he smiled a faint smile which intimated his opinion of the donor's *savoir faire*—he proceeded to call a coach. To the driver he also recommended me, giving at the same time an injunction about taking me, I think, to the wharf, and not leaving me to the watermen; which that functionary promised to observe, but failed in keeping his promise: on the contrary, he offered me up as an oblation, served me as a dripping roast, making me alight in the midst of a throng of watermen.

This was an uncomfortable crisis. It was a dark night. The coachman instantly drove off as soon as he had got his fare; the watermen commenced a struggle for me and my trunk. Their oaths I hear at this moment: they shook my philosophy more than did the night, or the isolation, or the strangeness of the scene. One laid hands on my trunk. I looked on and waited quietly; but when another laid hands on me I spoke up, shook off his touch, stepped at once into a boat, desired austerely that the trunk should be placed beside me—"Just there,"—which was instantly done; for the owner of the boat I had chosen became now an ally: I was rowed off.

Black was the river as a torrent of ink; lights glanced on it from the piles of building round, ships rocked on its bosom. They rowed me up to several vessels; I read by lantern-light their names painted in great, white letters on a dark ground. The *Ocean*, the *Phœnix*, the

Consort, the *Dolphin,* were passed in turns; but the *Vivid* was my ship, and it seemed she lay further down.

Down the sable flood we glided; I thought of the Styx, and of Charon rowing some solitary soul to the Land of Shades. Amidst the strange scene, with a chilly wind blowing in my face and midnight-clouds dropping rain above my head; with two rude rowers for companions, whose insane oaths still tortured my ear, I asked myself if I was wretched or terrified. I was neither. Often in my life have I been far more so under comparatively safe circumstances. "How is this?" said I. "Methinks I am animated and alert, instead of being depressed and apprehensive?" I could not tell how it was.

The "*Vivid*" started out, white and glaring, from the black night at last. "Here you are!" said the waterman, and instantly demanded six shillings.

"You ask too much," I said. He drew off from the vessel and swore he would not embark me till I paid it. A young man, the steward as I found afterwards, was looking over the ship's side; he grinned a smile in anticipation of the coming contest; to disappoint him, I paid the money. Three times that afternoon I had given crowns where I should have given shillings; but I consoled myself with the reflection, "It is the price of experience."

"They've cheated you!" said the steward exultingly when I got on board. I answered phlegmatically that "I knew it," and went below.

A stout, handsome and showy woman was in the ladies' cabin. I asked to be shown my berth; she looked hard at me, muttered something about it being unusual for passengers to come on board at that hour, and seemed disposed to be less than civil. What a face she had—so comely—so insolent and so selfish!

"Now that I am on board, I shall certainly stay here," was my answer. "I will trouble you to show me my berth."

She complied, but sullenly. I took off my bonnet, arranged my things, and lay down. Some difficulties had been passed through; a sort of victory was won: my homeless, anchorless, unsupported mind had again leisure for a brief repose. Till the *Vivid* arrived in harbour, no further action would be required of me; but then.... Oh! I could not look forward. Harassed, exhausted, I lay in a half-trance.

The stewardess talked all night; not to me but to the young steward, her son and her very picture. He passed in and out of the cabin continually: they disputed, they quarrelled, they made it up again twenty times in the course of the night. She professed to be writing a letter home—she said to her father; she read passages of it aloud, heeding me no more than a stock—perhaps she believed me asleep. Several of these passages appeared to comprise family secrets, and bore special reference to one "Charlotte," a younger sister who, from the bearing of the epistle, seemed to be on the brink of perpetrating a romantic and imprudent match; loud was the protest of this elder lady against the distasteful union. The dutiful son laughed his mother's correspondence to scorn. She defended it, and raved at him. They were a strange pair. She might be thirty-nine or forty, and was buxom and blooming as a girl of twenty. Hard, loud, vain and vulgar, her mind and body alike seemed brazen and imperishable. I should think, from her childhood, she must have lived in public stations; and in her youth might very likely have been a barmaid.

Towards morning her discourse ran on a new theme: "the Watsons," a certain expected family party of passengers, known to her, it appeared, and by her much esteemed on account of the handsome profit realised in their fees. She said, "it was as good as a little fortune to her whenever this family crossed."

At dawn all were astir, and by sunrise the passengers came on board. Boisterous was the welcome given by

the stewardess to the "Watsons," and great was the
bustle made in their honour. They were four in number,
two males and two females. Besides them, there was but
one other passenger—a young lady, whom a gentlemanly,
though languid-looking man escorted. The two groups
offered a marked contrast. The Watsons were doubtless
rich people, for they had the confidence of conscious
wealth in their bearing; the women—youthful both of
them, and one perfectly handsome, as far as physical
beauty went—were dressed richly, gaily, and absurdly
out of character for the circumstances. Their bonnets
with bright flowers, their velvet cloaks and silk dresses
seemed better suited for park or promenade than for
a damp packet deck. The men were of low stature, plain,
fat and vulgar; the oldest, plainest, greasiest, broadest,
I soon found was the husband—the bridegroom, I
suppose, for she was very young—of the beautiful girl.
Deep was my amazement at this discovery; and deeper
still when I perceived that, instead of being desperately
wretched in such a union, she was gay even to giddiness.
"Her laughter," I reflected, "must be the mere frenzy
of despair." And even while this thought was crossing
my mind, as I stood leaning quiet and solitary against
the ship's side, she came tripping up to me, an utter
stranger, with a camp stool in her hand, and smiling
a smile of which the levity puzzled and startled me,
though it showed a perfect set of perfect teeth, she offered
me the accommodation of this piece of furniture.
I declined it of course, with all the courtesy I could put
into my manner; she danced off heedless and lightsome.
She must have been good-natured; but what had made
her marry that individual, who was at least as much like
an oil-barrel as a man?

The other lady passenger, with the gentleman companion, was quite a girl, pretty and fair: her simple print
dress, untrimmed straw bonnet and large shawl, grace-
fully worn, formed a costume plain to quakerism: yet,

for her, becoming enough. Before the gentleman quitted her, I observed him throwing a glance of scrutiny over all the passengers, as if to ascertain in what company his charge would be left. With a most dissatisfied air did his eye turn from the ladies with the gay flowers; he looked at me, and then he spoke to his daughter, niece, or whatever she was: she also glanced in my direction, and slightly curled her short, pretty lip. It might be myself, or it might be my homely mourning habit, that elicited this mark of contempt; more likely, both. A bell rang; her father (I afterwards knew that it was her father) kissed her, and returned to land. The packet sailed.

Foreigners say that it is only English girls who can thus be trusted to travel alone, and deep is their wonder at the daring confidence of English parents and guardians. As for the "jeunes Miss," by some their intrepidity is pronounced masculine and "inconvenant," others regard them as the passive victims of an educational and theological system which wantonly dispenses with proper "surveillance." Whether this particular young lady was of the sort that can the most safely be left unwatched, I do not know: or rather did not *then* know; but it soon appeared that the dignity of solitude was not to her taste. She paced the deck once or twice backwards and for-wards; she looked with a little sour air of disdain at the flaunting silks and velvets, and the bears which thereon danced attendance, and eventually she approached me and spoke.

"Are you fond of a sea voyage?" was her question.

I explained that my *fondness* for a sea voyage had yet to undergo the test of experience; I had never made one.

"Oh, how charming!" cried she. "I quite envy you the novelty: first impressions, you know, are so pleasant. Now I have made so many, I quite forget the first: I am quite *blasée* about the sea and all that."

I could not help smiling.

"Why do you laugh at me?" she inquired, with a frank testiness that pleased me better than her other talk.

"Because you are so young to be *blasée* about anything."

"I am seventeen" (a little piqued).

"You hardly look sixteen. Do you like travelling alone?"

"Bah! I care nothing about it. I have crossed the Channel ten times, alone; but then I take care never to be long alone; I always make friends."

"You will scarcely make many friends this voyage, I think" (glancing at the Watson group, who were now laughing and making a great deal of noise on deck).

"Not of those odious men and women," said she: "such people should be steerage passengers. Are you going to school?"

"No."

"Where are you going?"

"I have not the least idea—beyond, at least, the Port of Boue-Marine."

She stared, then carelessly ran on:

"I am going to school. Oh the number of foreign schools I have been at in my life! And yet I am quite an ignoramus. I know nothing—nothing in the world— I assure you; except that I play and dance beautifully,— and French and German of course I know, to speak; but I can't read or write them very well. Do you know they wanted me to translate a page of an easy German book into English the other day, and I couldn't do it. Papa was so mortified: he says it looks as if M. de Bassompierre —my godpapa, who pays all my school-bills—had thrown away all his money. And then, in matters of information —in history, geography, arithmetic, and so on, I am quite a baby; and I write English so badly—such spelling and grammar, they tell me. Into the bargain I have quite forgotten my religion; they call me a Protestant, you know, but really I am not sure whether I am one or not: I don't well know the difference between Romanism and Protestantism. However, I don't in the least care for that. I was a Lutheran once at Bonn—dear Bonn!— charming Bonn!—where there were so many handsome students. Every nice girl in our school had an admirer; they knew our hours for walking out, and almost always passed us on the promenade: 'Schönes Mädchen,' we used to hear them say. I was excessively happy at Bonn!"

"And where are you now?" I inquired.

"Oh! at—*chose*," said she.

Now, Miss Ginevra Fanshawe (such was this young person's name) only substituted this word "*chose*" in temporary oblivion of the real name. It was a habit she had: "*chose*" came in at every turn in her conversation— the convenient substitute for any missing word in any language she might chance at the time to be speaking. French girls often do the like; from them she caught the custom. "*Chose*," however, I found in this instance, stood for Villette—the great capital of the great kingdom of Labassecour.

"Do you like Villette?" I asked.

"Pretty well. The natives, you know, are intensely stupid and vulgar; but there are some nice English families."

"Are you in a school?"

"Yes."

"A good one?"

"Oh no! horrid: but I go out every Sunday, and care nothing about the *maîtresses* or the *professeurs*, or the *élèves*, and send lessons *au diable*; (one daren't say that in English, you know, but it sounds quite right in French), and thus I get on charmingly....You are laughing at me again?"

"No—I am only smiling at my own thoughts."

"What are they?" (without waiting for an answer)— "Now, *do* tell me where you are going."

"Where Fate may lead me. My business is to earn a living where I can find it."

"To earn!" (in consternation) "are you poor, then?"

"As poor as Job."

(After a pause) "Bah! how unpleasant! But *I* know what it is to be poor: they are poor enough at home—papa and mamma, and all of them. Papa is called Captain Fanshawe; he is an officer on half-pay, but well descended, and some of our connections are great enough; but my uncle and godpapa De Bassompierre, who lives in France, is the only one that helps us: he educates us girls. I have five sisters and three brothers. By-and-by we are to marry—rather elderly gentlemen, I suppose, with cash: papa and mamma manage that. My sister Augusta is married now to a man much older looking than papa. Augusta is very beautiful—not in my style—but dark; her husband, Mr Davies, had the yellow fever in India, and he is still the colour of a guinea; but then he is rich, and Augusta has her carriage and establishment, and we all think she has done perfectly well. Now, this is better than 'earning a living,' as you say. By the way, are you clever?"

"No—not at all."

"You can play, sing, speak three or four languages?"

"By no means."

"Still I think you are clever" (a pause and a yawn). "Shall you be sea-sick?"

"Shall you?"

"Oh, immensely! as soon as ever we get in sight of the sea: I begin, indeed, to feel it already. I shall go below; and won't I order about that fat odious stewardess. Heureusement je sais faire aller mon monde." Down she went.

It was not long before the other passengers followed her: throughout the afternoon I remained on deck alone. When I recall the tranquil, and even happy mood in which I passed those hours, and remember, at the same

time, the position in which I was placed: its hazardous
—some would have said its hopeless—character; I feel
that, as—

> Stone walls do not a prison make,
> Nor iron bars—a cage,

so peril, loneliness, an uncertain future, are not oppressive
evils, so long as the frame is healthy and the faculties are
employed; so long, especially, as Liberty lends us her
wings, and Hope guides us by her star.

I was not sick till long after we passed Margate, and
deep was the pleasure I drank in with the sea breeze;
divine the delight I drew from the heaving channel
waves, from the sea-birds on their ridges, from the white
sails on their dark distance, from the quiet yet beclouded
sky, overhanging all. In my reverie, methought I saw
the continent of Europe, like a wide dreamland, far away.
Sunshine lay on it, making the long coast one line of gold;
tiniest tracery of clustered town and snow-gleaming
tower, of woods deep massed, of heights serrated, of
smooth pasturage and veiny stream, embossed the metal-
bright prospect. For background, spread a sky, solemn
and dark blue, and—grand with imperial promise, soft
with tints of enchantment—strode from north to south
a God-bent bow, an arch of hope.

Cancel the whole of that, if you please, reader—or
rather let it stand, and draw thence a moral—an allitera-
tive, text-hand copy—

> Day-dreams are delusions of the demon.

Becoming excessively sick, I faltered down into the
cabin.

Miss Fanshawe's berth chanced to be next mine; and,
I am sorry to say, she tormented me with an unsparing
selfishness during the whole time of our mutual distress.
Nothing could exceed her impatience and fretfulness.
The Watsons, who were very sick too, and on whom the
stewardess attended with shameless partiality, were stoics

compared with her. Many a time since have I noticed, in persons of Ginevra Fanshawe's light, careless temperament, and fair, fragile style of beauty, an entire incapacity to endure; they seem to sour in adversity, like small beer in thunder. The man who takes such a woman for his wife, ought to be prepared to guarantee her an existence all sunshine. Indignant at last with her teasing peevishness, I curtly requested her "to hold her tongue." The rebuff did her good, and it was observable that she liked me no worse for it.

As dark night drew on, the sea roughened; larger waves swayed strong against the vessel's side. It was strange to reflect that blackness and water were round us, and to feel the ship ploughing straight on her pathless way, despite noise, billow and rising gale. Articles of furniture began to fall about, and it became needful to lash them to their places; the passengers grew sicker than ever; Miss Fanshawe declared, with groans, that she must die.

"Not just yet, honey," said the stewardess. "We're just in port." Accordingly, in another quarter of an hour, a calm fell upon us all; and about midnight the voyage ended.

I was sorry: yes, I was sorry. My resting time was past; my difficulties—my stringent difficulties—recommenced. When I went on deck, the cold air and black scowl of the night seemed to rebuke me for my presumption in being where I was: the lights of the foreign seaport town, glimmering round the foreign harbour, met me like unnumbered threatening eyes. Friends came on board to welcome the Watsons; a whole family of friends surrounded and bore away Miss Fanshawe; I—but I dared not for one moment dwell on a comparison of positions.

Yet where should I go? I must go somewhere. Necessity dare not be nice. As I gave the stewardess her fee—and she seemed surprised at receiving a coin of more value than, from such a quarter, her coarse calculations had probably reckoned on—I said:

"Be kind enough to direct me to some quiet, respectable inn, where I can go for the night."

She not only gave me the required direction, but called a commissionaire, and bid him take charge of me, and —*not* my trunk, for that was gone to the custom-house.

I followed this man along a rudely-paved street, lit now by a fitful gleam of moonlight; he brought me to the inn. I offered him sixpence, which he refused to take; supposing it not enough, I changed it for a shilling; but this also he declined, speaking rather sharply, in a language to me unknown. A waiter, coming forward into the lamp-lit inn passage, reminded me, in broken English, that my money was foreign money, not current here. I gave him a sovereign to change. This little matter settled, I asked for a bedroom; supper I could not take; I was still sea-sick and unnerved, and trembling all over. How deeply glad I was when the door of a very small chamber at length closed on me and my exhaustion. Again I might rest: though the cloud of doubt would be as thick to-morrow as ever; the necessity for exertion more urgent, the peril (of destitution) nearer, the conflict (for existence) more severe.

I awoke next morning with courage revived and spirits refreshed: physical debility no longer enervated my judgment; my mind felt prompt and clear.

Just as I finished dressing, a tap came to the door; I said, "Come in," expecting the chambermaid, whereas a rough man walked in and said—

"Gif me your keys, Meess."

"Why?" I asked.

"Gif!" said he impatiently; and as he half-snatched them from my hand, he added, "All right! haf your tronc soon."

Fortunately it did turn out all right: he was from the custom-house. Where to go to get some breakfast I could not tell; but I proceeded, not without hesitation, to descend.

I now observed, what I had not noticed in my extreme weariness last night, viz., that this inn was, in fact, a large hotel; and as I slowly descended the broad staircase, halting on each step (for I was in wonderfully little haste to get down), I gazed at the high ceiling above me, at the painted walls around, at the wide windows which filled the house with light, at the veined marble I trod (for the steps were all of marble, though uncarpeted and not very clean), and contrasting all this with the dimensions of the closet assigned to me as a chamber, with the extreme modesty of its appointments, I fell into a philosophising mood.

Much I marvelled at the sagacity evinced by waiters and chambermaids in proportioning the accommodation to the guest. How could inn servants and ship stewardesses everywhere tell at a glance that I, for instance, was an individual of no social significance and little burdened by cash? They *did* know it evidently: I saw quite well that they all, in a moment's calculation, estimated me at about the same fractional value. The fact seemed to me curious and pregnant; I would not disguise from myself what it indicated, yet managed to keep up my spirits pretty well under its pressure.

Having at last landed in a great hall, full of skylight glare, I made my way somehow to what proved to be the coffee-room. It cannot be denied that on entering this room I trembled somewhat; felt uncertain, solitary, wretched; wished to Heaven I knew whether I was doing right or wrong; felt convinced that it was the last, but could not help myself. Acting in the spirit and with the calm of a fatalist, I sat down at a small table, to which a waiter presently brought me some breakfast; and I partook of that meal in a frame of mind not greatly calculated to favour digestion. There were many other people breakfasting at other tables in the room; I should have felt rather more happy if amongst them all I could have seen any women; however, there was not one—all present were men. But nobody seemed to think I was doing anything strange; one or two gentlemen glanced at me occasionally, but none stared obtrusively; I suppose if there was anything eccentric in the business, they accounted for it by this word "Anglaise!"

Breakfast over, I must again move—in what direction? "Go to Villette," said an inward voice; prompted doubtless by the recollection of this slight sentence uttered carelessly and at random by Miss Fanshawe, as she bid me good-bye:

"I wish you would come to Madame Beck's; she has some marmots whom you might look after: she wants an English gouvernante, or was wanting one two months ago."

Who Madame Beck was, where she lived, I knew not; I had asked, but the question passed unheard; Miss Fanshawe, hurried away by her friends, left it unanswered. I presumed Villette to be her residence—to Villette I would go. The distance was forty miles. I knew I was catching at straws; but in the wide and weltering deep where I found myself, I would have caught at cobwebs. Having inquired about the means of travelling to Villette, and secured a seat in the diligence, I departed on the strength of this outline—this shadow of a project. Before you pronounce on the rashness of the proceeding, reader, look back to the point whence I started; consider the desert I had left, note how little I perilled: mine was the game where the player cannot lose and may win.

Of an artistic temperament I deny that I am; yet I must possess something of the artist's faculty of making the most of present pleasure: that is to say, when it is of the kind to my taste. I enjoyed that day, though we travelled slowly, though it was cold, though it rained. Somewhat bare, flat, and treeless was the route along which our journey lay; and slimy canals crept, like half-

torpid green snakes, beside the road; and formal pollard
willows edged level fields, tilled like kitchen-garden beds.
The sky, too, was monotonously gray; the atmosphere
was stagnant and humid; yet amidst all these deadening
influences, my fancy budded fresh and my heart basked
in sunshine. These feelings, however, were well kept in
check by the secret but ceaseless consciousness of anxiety
lying in wait on enjoyment, like a tiger crouched in
a jungle. The breathing of that beast of prey was in my
ear always; his fierce heart panted close against mine;
he never stirred in his lair but I felt him: I knew he
waited only for sundown to bound ravenous from his
ambush.

I had hoped we might reach Villette ere night set in,
and that thus I might escape the deeper embarrassment
which obscurity seems to throw round a first arrival at
an unknown bourne; but, what with our slow progress
and long stoppages—what with a thick fog and small,
dense rain—darkness, that might almost be felt, had
settled on the city by the time we gained its suburbs.

I know we passed through a gate where soldiers were
stationed—so much I could see by lamplight; then,
having left behind us the miry Chaussée, we rattled over
a pavement of strangely rough and flinty surface. At
a bureau, the diligence stopped, and the passengers
alighted. My first business was to get my trunk: a small
matter enough, but important to me. Understanding
that it was best not to be importunate or over eager about
luggage, but to wait and watch quietly the delivery of
other boxes till I saw my own, and then promptly claim
and secure it, I stood apart; my eye fixed on that part
of the vehicle in which I had seen my little portmanteau
safely stowed, and upon which piles of additional bags
and boxes were now heaped. One by one, I saw these
removed, lowered and seized on. I was sure mine ought
to be by this time visible: it was not. I had tied on the
direction card with a piece of green ribbon that I might

know it at a glance; not a fringe or fragment of green
was perceptible. Every package was removed; every
tin case and brown paper parcel; the oilcloth cover was
lifted; I saw with distinct vision that not an umbrella,
cloak, cane, hat-box or band-box remained.

And my portmanteau, with my few clothes and little
pocket-book enclasping the remnant of my fifteen pounds,
where were they?

I ask this question now, but I could not ask it then.
I could say nothing whatever; not possessing a phrase of
speaking French: and it was French, and French only,
the whole world seemed now gabbling around me. *What*
should I do? Approaching the conductor, I just laid
my hand on his arm, pointed to a trunk, thence to the
diligence roof, and tried to express a question with my
eyes. He misunderstood me, seized the trunk indicated,
and was about to hoist it on the vehicle.

"Let that alone—will you?" said a voice in good
English; then, in correction, "Qu'est ce que vous faîtes
donc? Cette malle est à moi."

But I had heard the fatherland accents; they rejoiced
my heart; I turned:

"Sir," said I, appealing to the stranger, without, in
my distress, noticing what he was like, "I cannot speak
French. May I entreat you to ask this man what he has
done with my trunk?"

Without discriminating for the moment what sort of
face it was to which my eyes were raised and on which
they were fixed, I felt in its expression half-surprise at
my appeal and half-doubt of the wisdom of interference.

"*Do* ask him; I would do as much for you," said I.

I don't know whether he smiled, but he said in a
gentlemanly tone; that is to say, a tone not hard nor
terrifying—

"What sort of trunk was yours?"

I described it, including in my description the green
ribbon. And forthwith he took the conductor under

hand, and I felt, through all the storm of French which followed, that he raked him fore and aft. Presently he returned to me.

"The fellow avers he was overloaded, and confesses that he removed your trunk after you saw it put on, and has left it behind at Boue-Marine with other parcels; he has promised, however, to forward it to-morrow; the day after, therefore, you will find it safe at this bureau."

"Thank you," said I: but my heart sank.

Meantime what should I do? Perhaps this English gentleman saw the failure of courage in my face; he inquired kindly:

"Have you any friends in this city?"

"No, and I don't know where to go."

There was a little pause, in the course of which, as he turned more fully to the light of a lamp above him, I saw that he was a young, distinguished and handsome man; he might be a lord for anything I knew; nature had made him good enough for a prince, I thought. His face was very pleasant; he looked high but not arrogant, manly but not overbearing. I was turning away, in the deep consciousness of all absence of claim to look for further help from such a one as he.

"Was all your money in your trunk?" he asked, stopping me.

How thankful was I to be able to answer with truth—

"No. I have enough in my purse" (for I had near twenty francs) "to keep me at a quiet inn till the day after to-morrow; but I am quite a stranger in Villette, and don't know the streets and the inns."

"I can give you the address of such an inn as you want," said he; "and it is not far off; with my direction you will easily find it."

He tore a leaf from his pocket-book, wrote a few words and gave it to me. I *did* think him kind; and as to distrusting him, or his advice, or his address, I should almost as soon have thought of distrusting the Bible.

There was goodness in his countenance, and honour in his bright eyes.

"Your shortest way will be to follow the Boulevard and cross the park," he continued; "but it is too late and too dark for a woman to go through the park alone; I will step with you thus far."

He moved on, and I followed him, through the darkness and the small soaking rain. The Boulevard was all deserted, its path miry, the water dripping from its trees; the park was black as midnight. In the double gloom of trees and fog, I could not see my guide; I could only follow his tread. Not the least fear had I. I believe I would have followed that frank tread, through continual night, to the world's end.

"Now," said he, when the park was traversed, "you will go along this broad street till you come to steps; two lamps will show you where they are: these steps you will descend: a narrower street lies below; following that, at the bottom you will find your inn. They speak English there, so your difficulties are now pretty well over. Good-night."

"Good-night, sir," said I; "accept my sincerest thanks." And we parted....

I came at last to an old and worn flight, and, taking it for granted that this must be the one indicated, I descended them. The street into which they led was indeed narrow, but it contained no inn. On I wandered. In a very quiet and comparatively clean and well paved street, I saw a light burning over the door of a rather large house, loftier by a storey than those round it *This* might be the inn at last. I hastened on: my knees now trembled under me: I was getting quite exhausted.

No inn was this. A brass plate embellished the great portecochère: "Pensionnat de Demoiselles" was the inscription; and beneath, a name, "Madame Beck."

I started. About a hundred thoughts volleyed through my mind in a moment. Yet I planned nothing, and considered nothing: I had not time. Providence said, "Stop here; this is *your* inn." Fate took me in her strong hand; mastered my will; directed my actions: I rang the door bell.

While I waited, I would not reflect. I fixedly looked at the street stones, where the door lamp shone, and counted them and noted their shapes, and the glitter of wet on their angles. I rang again. They opened at last. A bonne in a smart cap stood before me.

"May I see Madame Beck?" I inquired.

I believe if I had spoken French she would not have admitted me; but, as I spoke English, she concluded I was a foreign teacher come on business connected with the pensionnat, and, even at that late hour, she let me in, without a word of reluctance or a moment of hesitation.

The next moment I sat in a cold, glittering salon, with porcelain stove unlit, and gilded ornaments, and polished floor. A pendule on the mantel-piece struck nine o'clock.

A quarter of an hour passed. How fast beat every pulse in my frame! How I turned cold and hot by turns! I sat with my eyes fixed on the door—a great white folding-door, with gilt mouldings: I watched to see a leaf move and open. All had been quiet: not a mouse had stirred; the white doors were closed and motionless.

"You ayre Engliss?" said a voice at my elbow. I almost bounded, so unexpected was the sound; so certain had I been of solitude.

No ghost stood beside me, nor anything of spectral aspect; merely a motherly, dumpy little woman, in a large shawl, a wrapping-gown, and a clean, trim night-cap.

I said I was English, and immediately, without further prelude, we fell to a most remarkable conversation. Madame Beck (for Madame Beck it was—she had entered by a little door behind me, and, being shod with the shoes of silence, I had heard neither her entrance nor approach)—Madame Beck had exhausted her command of insular speech when she said "You ayre Engliss," and she now proceeded to work away volubly in her own tongue. I answered in mine. She partly understood me, but as I did not at all understand her—though we made together an awful clamour (anything like Madame's gift of utterance I had not hitherto heard or imagined)—we achieved little progress. She rang, ere long, for aid; which arrived in the shape of a "maîtresse," who had been partly educated in an Irish convent, and was esteemed a perfect adept in the English language. A bluff little personage this maîtresse was—Labassecourienne from top to toe: and how she did slaughter the speech of Albion! However, I told her a plain tale, which she translated. I told her how I had left my own country, intent on extending my knowledge, and gaining my bread; how I was ready to turn my hand to any useful thing, provided it was not wrong or degrading; how I would be a child's nurse, or a lady's-maid, and would not refuse even housework adapted to my strength. Madame heard this; and, questioning her countenance, I almost thought the tale won her ear.

"Il n'y a que les Anglaises pour ces sortes d'entreprises," said she: "sont-elles donc intrépides ces femmes là!"

She asked my name, my age; she sat and looked at me —not pityingly, not with interest: never a gleam of sympathy, or a shade of compassion, crossed her countenance during the interview. I felt she was not one to be led an inch by her feelings: grave and considerate, she gazed, consulting her judgment and studying my narrative. A bell rang.

"Voilà pour la prière du soir!" said she, and rose. Through her interpreter, she desired me to depart now, and come back on the morrow; but this did not suit me: I could not bear to return to the perils of darkness and the street. With energy, yet with a collected and controlled manner, I said, addressing herself personally, and not the maîtresse:

"Be assured, madame, that by instantly securing my services, your interests will be served and not injured: you will find me one who will wish to give, in her labour, a full equivalent for her wages; and if you hire me, it will be better that I should stay here this night: having no acquaintance in Villette, and not possessing the language of the country, how can I secure a lodging?"

"It is true," said she; "but at least you could give a reference?"

"None."

She inquired after my luggage: I told her when it would arrive. She mused. At that moment a man's step was heard in the vestibule, hastily proceeding to the outer door. (I shall go on with this part of my tale as if I had understood all that had passed; for though it was then scarce intelligible to me, I heard it translated afterwards.)

"Who goes out now?" demanded Madame Beck, listening to the tread.

"M. Paul," replied the teacher. "He came this evening to give a reading to the first class."

"The very man I should at this moment most wish to see. Call him."

The teacher ran to the saloon door. M. Paul was summoned. He entered: a small, dark and spare man, in spectacles.

"Mon cousin," began Madame, "I want your opinion. We know your skill in physiognomy; use it now. Read that countenance."

The little man fixed on me his spectacles. A resolute compression of the lips, and gathering of the brow, seemed to say that he meant to see through me, and that a veil would be no veil for him.

"I read it," he pronounced.

"Et qu'en dites vous?"

"Mais—bien des choses," was the oracular answer.

"Bad or good?"

"Of each kind, without doubt," pursued the diviner.

"May one trust her word?"

"Are you negotiating a matter of importance?"

"She wishes me to engage her as bonne or gouvernante; tells a tale full of integrity, but gives no reference."

"She is a stranger?"

"An Englishwoman, as one may see."

"She speaks French?"

"Not a word."

"She understands it?"

"No."

"One may then speak plainly in her presence?"

"Doubtless."

He gazed steadily. "Do you need her services?"

"I could do with them. You know I am disgusted with Madame Svini."

Still he scrutinised. The judgment, when it at last came, was as indefinite as what had gone before it.

"Engage her. If good predominates in that nature, the action will bring its own reward; if evil—eh bien! ma cousine, ce sera toujours une bonne œuvre." And with a bow and a "bon soir," this vague arbiter of my destiny vanished.

And Madame did engage me that very night—by God's blessing I was spared the necessity of passing forth again into the lonesome, dreary, hostile street.

A GLIMPSE OF THE PROFESSOR
BEHIND HIS SPECTACLES

from *Villette*.

M. PAUL EMANUEL owned an acute sensitiveness to the annoyance of interruption, from whatsoever cause occurring, during his lessons: to pass through the classe under such circumstances was considered by the teachers and pupils of the school, individually and collectively, to be as much as a woman's or girl's life was worth.

Madame Beck, herself, if forced to the enterprise, would "skurry" through, retrenching her skirts, and carefully coasting the formidable estrade, like a ship dreading breakers. As to Rosine, the portress—on whom, every half hour, devolved the fearful duty of fetching pupils out of the very heart of one or other of the divisions to take their music lessons in the oratory, the great or little saloon, the salle-à-manger, or some other piano station—she would, upon her second or third attempt, frequently become almost tongue-tied from excess of consternation—a sentiment inspired by the unspeakable looks levelled at her through a pair of dart-dealing spectacles.

One morning I was sitting in the carré, at work upon a piece of embroidery which one of the pupils had commenced but delayed to finish, and while my fingers wrought at the frame, my ears regaled themselves with listening to the crescendos and cadences of a voice haranguing in the neighbouring classe, in tones that waxed momentarily more unquiet, more ominously varied. There was a good strong partition wall between me and the gathering storm, as well as a facile means of flight through the glass door to the court, in case it swept this way; so I am afraid I derived more amusement than alarm from these thickening symptoms. Poor Rosine was not safe: four times that blessed morning had she made the passage of peril; and now, for the fifth time, it became her dangerous duty to snatch, as it were, a brand from the burning—a pupil from under M. Paul's nose.

"Mon Dieu! mon Dieu!" cried she. "Que vais-je devenir? Monsieur va me tuer, je suis sure; car il est d'une colère!"

Nerved by the courage of desperation, she opened the door.

"Mademoiselle La Malle au piano!" was her cry. Ere she could make good her retreat, or quite close the door, this voice uttered itself:

"Dès ce moment!—la classe est défendue. La première qui ouvrira cette porte, ou passera par cette division, sera pendue—fut-ce Madame Beck elle-même!"

Ten minutes had not succeeded the promulgation of this decree, when Rosine's French pantoufles were again heard shuffling along the corridor.

"Mademoiselle," said she, "I would not for a five-franc piece go into that classe again just now: Monsieur's lunettes are really terrible; and here is a commissionaire come with a message from the Athénée. I have told Madame Beck I dare not deliver it, and she says I am to charge you with it."

"Me? No, that is rather too bad! It is not in my line of duty. Come, come, Rosine! bear your own burden. Be brave—charge once more!"

"I, Mademoiselle?—impossible! Five times I have crossed him this day. Madame must really hire a gendarme for this service. Ouf! Je n'en puis plus!"

"Bah! you are only a coward. What is the message?"

"Precisely of the kind with which Monsieur least likes to be pestered: an urgent summons to go directly to the Athénée, as there is an official visitor—inspector—I know not what—arrived, and Monsieur *must* meet him: you know how he hates a *must*."

Yes, I knew well enough. The restless little man

detested spur or curb: against whatever was urgent or obligatory, he was sure to revolt. However, I accepted the responsibility—not, certainly, without fear; but fear blent with other sentiments, curiosity amongst them. I opened the door, I entered, I closed it behind me as quickly and quietly as a rather unsteady hand would permit; for to be slow or bustling, to rattle a latch, or leave a door gaping wide, were aggravations of crime often more disastrous in result than the main crime itself. There I stood then, and there he sat; his humour was visibly bad—almost at its worst; he had been giving a lesson in arithmetic—for he gave lessons on any and every subject that struck his fancy—and arithmetic being a dry subject, invariably disagreed with him: not a pupil but trembled when he spoke of figures. He sat, bent above his desk: to look up at the sound of an entrance, at the occurrence of a direct breach of his will and law, was an effort he could not for the moment bring himself to make. It was quite as well: I thus gained time to walk up the long classe; and it suited my idiosyncracy far better to encounter the near burst of anger like his, than to bear its menace at a distance.

At his estrade I paused, just in front; of course I was not worthy of immediate attention: he proceeded with his lesson. Disdain would not do: he must hear and he must answer my message.

Not being quite tall enough to lift my head over his desk, elevated upon the estrade, and thus suffering eclipse in my present position, I ventured to peep round, with the design, at first, of merely getting a better view of his face, which had struck me when I entered as bearing a close and picturesque resemblance to that of a black and sallow tiger. Twice did I enjoy this side view with impunity, advancing and receding unseen; the third time my eye had scarce dawned beyond the ob-scuration of the desk, when it was caught and transfixed through its very pupil—transfixed by the "lunettes."

Rosine was right; these utensils had in them a blank and immutable terror, beyond the mobile wrath of the wearer's own unglazed eyes.

I now found the advantage of proximity: these short-sighted "lunettes" were useless for the inspection of a criminal under Monsieur's nose; accordingly, he doffed them, and he and I stood on more equal terms.

I am glad I was not really much afraid of him—that, indeed, close in his presence, I felt no terror at all; for upon his demanding cord and gibbet to execute the sentence recently pronounced, I was able to furnish him with a needleful of embroidering thread with such accommodating civility as could not but allay some portion at least of his surplus irritation. Of course I did not parade this courtesy before public view; I merely handed the thread round the angle of the desk, and attached it, ready noosed, to the barred back of the Professor's chair.

"Que me voulez-vous?" said he in a growl of which the music was wholly confined to his chest and throat, for he kept his teeth clenched, and seemed registering to himself an inward vow that nothing earthly should wring from him a smile. My answer commenced un-comprisingly:

"Monsieur," I said, "je veux l'impossible, des choses inouies"; and thinking it best not to mince matters, but to administer the "douche" with decision, in a low but quick voice, I delivered the Athenian message, floridly exaggerating its urgency.

Of course, he would not hear a word of it. "He would not go; he would not leave his present class, let all the officials of Villette send for him. He would not put himself an inch out of his way at the bidding of king, cabinet and chambers together."

I knew, however, that he *must* go; that, talk as he would, both his duty and interest commanded an immediate and literal compliance with the summons: I stood, therefore, waiting in silence, as if he had not yet spoken. He asked what more I wanted.

"Only Monsieur's answer to deliver to the commissionaire."

He waved an impatient negative.

I ventured to stretch my hand to the bonnet-grec which lay in grim repose on the window-sill. He followed this daring movement with his eye, no doubt in mixed pity and amazement at its presumption.

"Ah!" he muttered, "if it came to that—if Miss Lucy meddled with his bonnet-grec—she might just put it on herself, turn garçon for the occasion, and benevolently go to the Athénée in his stead."

With great respect, I laid the bonnet on the desk, where its tassel seemed to give me an awful nod.

"I'll write a note of apology—that will do!" said he, still bent on evasion.

Knowing well it would *not* do, I gently pushed the bonnet towards his hand. Thus impelled, it slid down the polished slope of the varnished and unbaized desk, carried before it the light steel-framed "lunettes," and, fearful to relate, they fell to the estrade. A score of times ere now had I seen them fall and receive no damage— *this* time, as Lucy Snowe's hapless luck would have it, they so fell that each clear pebble became a shivered and shapeless star.

Now, indeed, dismay seized me—dismay and regret. I knew the value of these "lunettes"; M. Paul's sight was peculiar, not easily fitted, and these glasses suited him. I had heard him call them his treasures: as I picked them up, cracked and worthless, my hand trembled. Frightened through all my nerves I was to see the mischief I had done, but I think I was even more sorry than afraid. For some seconds I dared not look the bereaved Professor in the face; he was the first to speak.

"Là!" said he: "me voilà veuf de mes lunettes! I think Mademoiselle Lucy will now confess that the cord and gallows are amply earned; she trembles in anticipation of her doom. Ah, traitress! traitress! You are resolved to have me quite blind and helpless in your hands!"

I lifted my eyes: his face, instead of being irate, lowering and furrowed, was overflowing with the smile, coloured with the bloom I had seen brightening it that evening at the Hôtel Crécy. He was not angry—not even grieved. For the real injury he showed himself full of clemency; under the real provocation, patient as a saint. This event, which seemed so untoward—which I thought had ruined at once my chance of successful persuasion—proved my best help. Difficult of management so long as I had done him no harm, he became graciously pliant as soon as I stood in his presence a conscious and contrite offender.

Still gently railing at me as "une forte femme—une Anglaise terrible—une petite casse-tout"—he declared that he dared not but obey one who had given such an instance of her dangerous prowess; it was absolutely like the "grand Empereur smashing the vase to inspire dismay." So, at last, crowning himself with his bonnet-grec, and taking his ruined "lunettes" from my hand with a clasp of kind pardon and encouragement, he made his bow and went off to the Athénée in first-rate humour and spirits.

THE FAIRY MALEVOLA

from *Villette*.

MADAME BECK called me on Thursday afternoon, and asked whether I had any occupation to hinder me from going into town and executing some little commissions for her at the shops.

Being disengaged, and placing myself at her service, I was presently furnished with a list of the wools, silks, embroidering thread, et cetera, wanted in the pupils' work, and having equipped myself in a manner suiting the threatening aspect of a cloudy and sultry day, I was just drawing the spring-bolt of the street door, in act to issue forth, when Madame's voice again summoned me to the salle-à-manger.

"Pardon, Meess Lucie!" cried she, in the seeming haste of an impromptu thought, "I have just recollected one more errand for you, if your good nature will not deem itself overburdened?"

Of course I "confounded myself" in asseverations to the contrary; and Madame, running into the little salon, brought thence a pretty basket, filled with fine hothouse fruit, rosy, perfect and tempting, reposing amongst the dark green, wax-like leaves, and pale yellow stars of, I know not what, exotic plant.

"There," she said, "it is not heavy, and will not shame your neat toilette, as if it were a household, servant-like detail. Do me the favour to leave this little basket at the house of Madame Walravens, with my felicitations on her fête. She lives down in the old town, Numéro 3, Rue des Mages. I fear you will find the walk rather long, but you have the whole afternoon before you, and do not hurry; if you are not back in time for dinner, I will order a portion to be saved, or Goton, with whom you are a favourite, will have pleasure in tossing up some trifle for your especial benefit. You shall not be forgotten, ma bonne Meess. And oh! please!" (calling me back once more) "be sure to insist on seeing Madame Walravens herself, and giving the basket into her own hands, in order that there may be no mistake, for she is rather a punctilious personage. Adieu! Au revoir!"

And at last I got away. The shop commissions took some time to execute, that choosing and matching of silks and wools being always a tedious business, but at last I got through my list. The patterns for the slippers, the bell-ropes, the cabas were selected—the slides and tassels for the purses chosen—the whole "tripotage" in short, was off my mind; nothing but the fruit and the felicitations remained to be attended to.

I rather liked the prospect of a long walk, deep into the old and grim Basse-Ville; and I liked it no worse because the evening sky, over the city, was settling into a mass of black-blue metal, heated at the rim, and inflaming slowly to a heavy red.

I fear a high wind, because storm demands that exertion of strength and use of action I always yield with pain; but the sullen downfall, the thick snow descent, or dark rush of rain, ask only resignation—the quiet abandonment of garments and person to be drenched. In return, it sweeps a great capital clean before you; it makes you a quiet path through broad, grand streets; it petrifies a living city as if by eastern enchantment; it transforms a Villette into a Tadmor. Let, then, the rains fall, and the floods descend—only I must first get rid of this basket of fruit.

An unknown clock from an unknown tower (Jean Baptiste's voice was now too distant to be audible) was tolling the third quarter past five, when I reached that street and house whereof Madame Beck had given me the address. It was no street at all; it seemed rather to be part of a square; it was quiet, grass grew between the broad grey flags, the houses were large and looked very old—behind them rose the appearance of trees, indicating gardens at the back. Antiquity brooded above this region, business was banished thence. Rich men had once possessed this quarter, and once grandeur had made her seat here. That church, whose dark, half-ruinous turrets overlooked the square, was the venerable and formerly opulent shrine of the Magi. But wealth and greatness had long since stretched their gilded pinions and fled hence, leaving these their ancient nests, perhaps to house Penury for a time, or perhaps to stand cold and empty, mouldering untenanted in the course of winters.

As I crossed this deserted "place," on whose pavement drops almost as large as a five-franc piece were now slowly darkening, I saw, in its whole expanse, no symptom or evidence of life, except what was given in the figure of an infirm old priest, who went past, bending and propped on a staff—the type of eld and decay.

He had issued from the very house to which I was directed; and when I paused before the door just closed after him, and rang the bell, he turned to look at me. Nor did he soon avert his gaze; perhaps he thought me, with my basket of summer fruit, and my lack of the dignity age confers, an incongruous figure in such a scene. I know, had a young ruddy-faced bonne opened the door to admit me, I should have thought such a one little in harmony with her dwelling; but when I found myself confronted by a very old woman, wearing a very antique peasant costume, a cap alike hideous and costly, with long flaps of native lace, a petticoat and jacket of cloth, and sabots more like little boats than shoes, it seemed all right, and soothingly in character.

The expression of her face was not quite so soothing as the cut of her costume; anything more cantankerous I have seldom seen; she would scarcely reply to my inquiry after Madame Walravens; I believe she would have snatched the basket of fruit from my hand, had not the old priest, hobbling up, checked her, and himself lent an ear to the message with which I was charged.

His apparent deafness rendered it a little difficult to make him fully understand that I must see Madame Walravens, and consign the fruit into her own hands. At last, however, he comprehended the fact that such were my orders, and that duty enjoined their literal fulfilment. Addressing the aged bonne, not in French, but in the aboriginal tongue of Labassecour, he persuaded her, at last, to let me cross the inhospitable threshold, and himself escorting me upstairs, I was ushered into a sort of salon, and there left.

The room was large, and had a fine old ceiling, and almost church-like windows of coloured glass; but it was desolate, and in the shadow of a coming storm, looked strangely lowering. Within—opened a smaller room; there, however, the blind of the single casement was closed; through the deep gloom few details of furniture were apparent. These few I amused myself by puzzling to make out; and, in particular, I was attracted by the outline of a picture on the wall.

By-and-by the picture seemed to give way: to my bewilderment, it shook, it sunk, it rolled back into nothing; its vanishing left an opening arched, leading into an arched passage, with a mystic winding stair; both passage and stair were of cold stone, uncarpeted and unpainted. Down this donjon stair descended a tap, tap, like a stick; soon, there fell on the steps a shadow, and last of all, I was aware of a substance.

Yet, was it actual substance, this appearance approaching me? this obstruction, partially darkening the arch?

It drew near, and I saw it well. I began to comprehend where I was. Well might this old square be named quarter of the Magi—well might the three towers, overlooking it, own for godfathers three mystic sages of a dead and dark art. Hoar enchantment here prevailed; a spell had opened for me elf-land—that cell-like room, that vanishing picture, that arch and passage, and stair of stone, were all parts of a fairy tale. Distincter even than these scenic details stood the chief figure—Cunegonde, the sorceress! Malevola, the evil fairy. How was she?

She might be three feet high, but she had no shape; her skinny hands rested upon each other, and pressed the gold knob of a wand-like ivory staff. Her face was large, set, not upon her shoulders, but before her breast; she seemed to have no neck; I should have said there were a hundred years in her features, and more perhaps in her eyes—her malign, unfriendly eyes, with thick grey brows above, and livid lids all round. How severely they viewed me, with a sort of dull displeasure!

This being wore a gown of brocade, dyed bright blue, full-tinted as the gentianella flower, and covered with satin foliage in a large pattern; over the gown a costly shawl, gorgeously bordered, and so large for her, that its many-coloured fringe swept the floor. But her chief points were her jewels: she had long, clear earrings, blazing with a lustre which could not be borrowed or false; she had rings on her skeleton hands, with thick gold hoops, and stones—purple, green and blood-red. Hunchbacked, dwarfish, and doting, she was adorned like a barbarian queen.

"Que me voulez-vous?" said she, hoarsely, with the voice rather of male than of female old age; and, indeed, a silver beard bristled her chin.

I delivered my basket and my message.

"Is that all?" she demanded.

"It is all," said I.

"Truly, it was well worth while," she answered. "Return to Madame Beck, and tell her I can buy fruit when I want it, et quant à ses félicitations, je m'en moque!" And this courteous dame turned her back.

Just as she turned, a peal of thunder broke, and a flash of lightning blazed broad over salon and boudoir. The tale of magic seemed to proceed with due accompaniment of the elements. The wanderer, decoyed into the enchanted castle, heard rising, outside, the spell-wakened tempest.

What, in all this, was I to think of Madame Beck? She owned strange acquaintance; she offered messages and gifts to a unique shrine, and inauspicious seemed the bearing of the uncouth thing she worshipped. There went that sullen Sidonia, tottering and trembling like palsy incarnate, tapping her ivory staff on the mosaic parquet, and muttering venomously as she vanished.

Down washed the rain, deep lowered the welkin; the clouds, ruddy a while ago, had now, through all their blackness, turned deadly pale, as if in terror. Notwithstanding my late boast about not fearing a shower, I hardly liked to go out under this waterspout. Then the gleams of lightning were very fierce, the thunder crashed very near; this storm had gathered immediately above Villette; it seemed to have burst at the zenith; it rushed down prone; the forked, slant bolts pierced athwart vertical torrents; red zig-zags interlaced a descent blanched as white metal; and all broke from a sky heavily black in its swollen abundance.

Leaving Madame Walravens' inhospitable salon, I betook myself to her cold staircase; there was a seat on the landing—there I waited. Somebody came gliding along the gallery just above; it was the old priest.

"Indeed mademoiselle shall not sit there," said he. "It would displeasure our benefactor if he knew a stranger was so treated in this house."

And he begged me so earnestly to return to the salon, that, without discourtesy, I could not but comply. The smaller room was better furnished and more habitable than the larger; thither he introduced me. Partially withdrawing the blind, he disclosed what seemed more like an oratory than a boudoir, a very solemn little chamber, looking as if it were a place rather dedicated to relics and remembrance, than designed for present use and comfort.

The good father sat down, as if to keep me company; but instead of conversing, he took out a book, fastened on the page his eyes, and employed his lips in whispering—what sounded like a prayer or litany. A yellow electric light from the sky gilded his bald head; his figure remained in shade—deep and purple; he sat still as sculpture; he seemed to forget me for his prayers; he only looked up when a fiercer bolt, or a harsher, closer rattle told of nearing danger; even then, it was not in

fear, but in seeming awe, he raised his eyes. I too was
awe-struck; being, however, under no pressure of slavish
terror, my thoughts and observations were free....

Beside a cross of curiously carved old ivory, yellow
with time, and sloped above a dark red *prie-dieu,* furnished
duly with rich missal and ebon rosary—hung the picture
whose dim outline had drawn my eyes before—the
picture which moved, fell away with the wall and let in
phantoms. Imperfectly seen, I had taken it for a Ma-
donna; revealed by clearer light, it proved to be a
woman's portrait in a nun's dress. The face, though not
beautiful, was pleasing; pale, young, and shaded with
the dejection of grief or ill-health. I say again it was not
beautiful; it was not even intellectual; its very amiability
was the amiability of a weak frame, inactive passions,
acquiescent habits: yet I looked long at that picture, and
could not choose but look.

The old priest, who at first had seemed to me so deaf
and infirm, must yet have retained his faculties in tolerable preservation; absorbed in his book as he appeared,
without once lifting his head, or, as far as I knew, turning
his eyes, he perceived the point towards which my
attention was drawn, and, in a slow distinct voice,
dropped concerning it, these four observations:

"She was much beloved.

"She gave herself to God.

"She died young.

"She is still remembered, still wept."

"By that aged lady, Madame Walravens?" I inquired,
fancying that I had discovered, in the incurable grief of
bereavement, a key to that same aged lady's desperate
humour.

The father shook his head with half a smile.

"No, no," said he; "a grand-dame's affection for her
children's children may be great, and her sorrow for
their loss, lively; but it is only the affianced lover, to
whom Fate, Faith and Death, have trebly denied the

bliss of union, who mourns what he has lost, as Justine
Marie is still mourned."

I thought the father rather wished to be questioned, and
therefore I inquired who had lost and who still mourned
"Justine Marie." I got, in reply, quite a little romantic
narrative, told not unimpressively, with the accompaniment of the now subsiding storm. I am bound to say it
might have been made much more truly impressive, if
there had been less French, Rousseau-like sentimentalis-
ing and wire-drawing; and rather more healthful carelessness of effect. But the worthy father was obviously
a Frenchman born and bred (I became more and more
persuaded of his resemblance to my confessor)—he was
a true son of Rome; when he did lift his eyes, he looked
at me out of their corners, with more and sharper
subtlety than, one would have thought, could survive
the wear and tear of seventy years. Yet, I believe, he
was a good old man.

The hero of his tale was some former pupil of his, whom
he now called his benefactor, and who, it appears, had
loved this pale Justine Marie, the daughter of rich
parents, at a time when his own worldly prospects were
such as to justify his aspiring to a well-dowered hand.
The pupil's father—once a rich banker—had failed, died,
and left behind him only debts and destitution. The son
was then forbidden to think of Marie, especially that old
witch of a grand-dame I had seen, Madame Walravens,
opposed the match with all the violence of a temper
which deformity made sometimes demoniac. The mild
Marie had neither the treachery to be false, nor the force
to be quite staunch to her lover; she gave up her first
suitor, but, refusing to accept a second with a heavier purse,
withdrew to a convent, and there died in her noviciate.

Lasting anguish, it seems, had taken possession of the
faithful heart which worshipped her, and the truth of
that love and grief had been shown in a manner which
touched even me, as I listened.

Some years after Justine Marie's death, ruin had come on her house too; her father, by nominal calling a jeweller, but who also dealt a good deal on the Bourse, had been concerned in some financial transactions which entailed exposure and ruinous fines. He died of grief for the loss, and shame for the infamy. His old hunch-backed mother and his bereaved wife were left penniless, and might have died too of want; but their lost daughter's once-despised, yet most true-hearted suitor, hearing of the condition of these ladies, came with singular devotedness to the rescue. He took on their insolent pride the revenge of the purest charity—housing, caring for, befriending them, so as no son could have done it more tenderly and efficiently. The mother—on the whole a good woman—died blessing him; the strange, godless, loveless, misanthrope grandmother lived still, entirely supported by this self-sacrificing man. She who had been the bane of his life, blighting his hope, and awarding him, for love and domestic happiness, long mourning and cheerless solitude, he treated with the respect a good son might offer a kind mother. He had brought her to this house, "and," continued the priest, while genuine tears rose to his eyes, "here, too, he shelters me, his old tutor, and Agnes, a superannuated servant of his father's family. To our sustenance, and to other charities, I know he devotes three parts of his income, keeping only the fourth to provide himself with bread and the most modest accommodations. By this arrangement he has rendered it impossible to himself ever to marry: he has given himself to God and to his angel-bride as much as if he were a priest, like me.". . .

Perhaps the musing fit into which I had by this time fallen, appeared somewhat suspicious in its abstraction; he gently interrupted:

"Mademoiselle," said he, "I trust you have not far to go through these inundated streets?"

"More than half a league."

"You live——?"

"In the Rue Fossette."

"Not" (with animation), "not at the pensionnat of Madame Beck?"

"The same."

"Donc" (clapping his hands), "donc, vous devez connaître mon noble élève, mon Paul?"

"Monsieur Paul Emanuel, Professor of Literature?"

"He, and none other."

A brief silence fell. The spring of junction seemed suddenly to have become palpable; I felt it yield to pressure.

"Was it of M. Paul you have been speaking?" I presently inquired. "Was he your pupil and the benefactor of Madame Walravens?"

"Yes, and of Agnes, the old servant: and moreover" (with a certain emphasis), "he was and *is* the lover, true, constant and eternal, of that saint in heaven—Justine Marie."

A JOURNEY, AND THE FIRST DAY
AT LOWOOD

from *Jane Eyre*.

FIVE o'clock had hardly struck on the morning of the 19th of January, when Bessie brought a candle into my closet and found me already up and nearly dressed. I had risen half an hour before her entrance, and had washed my face, and put on my clothes by the light of a half-moon just setting, whose rays streamed through the narrow window near my crib. I was to leave Gateshead that day by a coach which passed the lodge gates at six a.m. Bessie was the only person yet risen; she had lit a fire in the nursery, where she now proceeded to make my breakfast. Few children can eat when excited with the thoughts of a journey; nor could I. Bessie, having pressed me in vain to take a few spoonfuls of the boiled milk and bread she had prepared for me, wrapped up some biscuits in a paper and put them into my bag; then she helped me on with my pelisse and bonnet, and wrapping herself in a shawl, she and I left the nursery....

"Good-bye to Gateshead!" cried I, as we passed through the hall and went out at the front door.

The moon was set, and it was very dark; Bessie carried a lantern, whose light glanced on wet steps and gravel road sodden by a recent thaw. Raw and chill was the winter morning: my teeth chattered as I hastened down the drive. There was a light in the porter's lodge: when we reached it, we found the porter's wife just kindling her fire: my trunk, which had been carried down the evening before, stood corded at the door. It wanted but a few minutes of six, and shortly after that hour had struck, the distant roll of wheels announced the coming coach; I went to the door and watched its lamps approach rapidly through the gloom.

"Is she going by herself?" asked the porter's wife.

"Yes."

"And how far is it?"

"Fifty miles."

"What a long way! I wonder Mrs Reed is not afraid to trust her so far alone."

The coach drew up; there it was at the gates with its four horses and its top laden with passengers: the guard and coachman loudly urged haste; my trunk was hoisted up; I was taken from Bessie's neck, to which I clung with kisses.

"Be sure and take good care of her," cried she to the guard, as he lifted me into the inside.

"Ay, ay!" was the answer: the door was slapped to, a voice exclaimed "All right," and on we drove. Thus was I severed from Bessie and Gateshead; thus whirled away to unknown, and, as I then deemed, remote and mysterious regions.

I remember but little of the journey; I only know that the day seemed to me of a preternatural length, and that we appeared to travel over hundreds of miles of road. We passed through several towns, and in one, a very large one, the coach stopped; the horses were taken out, and the passengers alighted to dine. I was carried into an inn, where the guard wanted me to have some dinner; but, as I had no appetite, he left me in an immense room with a fireplace at each end, a chandelier pendent from the ceiling, and a little red gallery high up against the wall filled with musical instruments. Here I walked about for a long time, feeling very strange, and mortally apprehensive of some one coming in and kidnapping me; for I believed in kidnappers, their exploits having frequently figured in Bessie's fireside chronicles. At last the guard returned; once more I was stowed away in the coach, my protector mounted his own seat, sounded his hollow horn, and away we rattled over the "stony street" of L——.

The afternoon came on wet and somewhat misty: as it waned into dusk, I began to feel that we were getting very far indeed from Gateshead: we ceased to pass through towns; the country changed; great grey hills heaved up round the horizon: as twilight deepened, we descended a valley, dark with wood, and long after night had overclouded the prospect, I heard a wild wind rushing amongst trees.

Lulled by the sound, I at last dropped asleep; I had not long slumbered when the sudden cessation of motion awoke me; the coach-door was open, and a person like a servant was standing at it: I saw her face and dress by the light of the lamps.

"Is there a little girl called Jane Eyre here?" she asked. I answered "Yes," and was then lifted out; my trunk was handed down, and the coach instantly drove away.

I was stiff with long sitting, and bewildered with the noise and motion of the coach: gathering my faculties,

I looked about me. Rain, wind, and darkness filled the air; nevertheless, I dimly discerned a wall before me and a door open in it; through this door I passed with my new guide: she shut and locked it behind her. There was now visible a house or houses—for the building spread far—with many windows, and lights burning in some; we went up a broad pebbly path, splashing wet, and were admitted at a door; then the servant led me through a passage into a room with a fire, where she left me alone.

I stood and warmed my numbed fingers over the blaze, then I looked round; there was no candle, but the uncertain light from the hearth showed, by intervals, papered walls, carpet, curtains, shining mahogany furniture: it was a parlour, not so spacious or splendid as the drawing-room at Gateshead, but comfortable enough. I was puzzling to make out the subject of a picture on the wall, when the door opened, and an individual carrying a light entered; another followed close behind.

The first was a tall lady with dark hair, dark eyes, and a pale and large forehead; her figure was partly enveloped in a shawl, her countenance was grave, her bearing erect.

"The child is very young to be sent alone," said she, putting her candle down on the table. She considered me attentively for a minute or two, then further added—

"She had better be put to bed soon; she looks tired: are you tired?" she asked, placing her hand on my shoulder.

"A little, ma'am."

"And hungry too, no doubt: let her have some supper before she goes to bed, Miss Miller. Is this the first time you have left your parents to come to school, my little girl?"

I explained to her that I had no parents. She inquired how long they had been dead: then how old I was, what was my name, whether I could read, write, and sew

a little: then she touched my cheek gently with her fore-
finger, and saying, "She hoped I should be a good
child," dismissed me along with Miss Miller.

The lady I had left might be about twenty-nine; the
one who went with me appeared some years younger:
the first impressed me by her voice, look, and air. Miss
Miller was more ordinary; ruddy in complexion, though
of a careworn countenance; hurried in gait and action,
like one who had always a multiplicity of tasks on hand:
she looked, indeed, what I afterwards found she really
was, an under-teacher. Led by her, I passed from compartment to compartment, from passage to passage, of
a large and irregular building; till, emerging from the
total and somewhat dreary silence pervading that portion
of the house we had traversed, we came upon the hum
of many voices, and presently entered a wide, long room,
with great deal tables, two at each end, on each of which
burnt a pair of candles, and seated all round on benches,
a congregation of girls of every age, from nine or ten to
twenty. Seen by the dim light of the dips, their number
to me appeared countless, though not in reality exceeding
eighty; they were uniformly dressed in brown stuff frocks
of quaint fashion, and long holland pinafores. It was
the hour of study; they were engaged in conning over
their to-morrow's task, and the hum I had heard was the
combined result of their whispered repetitions.

Miss Miller signed to me to sit on a bench near the
door, then walking up to the top of the long room she
cried out—

"Monitors, collect the lesson-books and put them
away!"

Four tall girls arose from different tables, and going
round, gathered the books and removed them. Miss
Miller again gave the word of command—

"Monitors, fetch the supper-trays!"

The tall girls went out and returned presently, each
bearing a tray, with portions of something, I knew not

what, arranged thereon, and a pitcher of water and mug in the middle of each tray. The portions were handed round; those who liked took a draught of the water, the mug being common to all. When it came to my turn, I drank, for I was thirsty, but did not touch the food, excitement and fatigue rendering me incapable of eating; I now saw, however, that it was a thin oaten cake shared into fragments.

The meal over, prayers were read by Miss Miller, and the classes filed off, two and two, upstairs. Overpowered by this time with weariness, I scarcely noticed what sort of a place the bedroom was, except that, like the schoolroom, I saw it was very long. To-night I was to be Miss Miller's bed-fellow; she helped me to undress: when laid down I glanced at the long rows of beds, each of which was quickly filled with two occupants; in ten minutes the single light was extinguished, and amidst silence and complete darkness I fell asleep.

The night passed rapidly: I was too tired even to dream; I only once awoke to hear the wind rave in furious gusts, and the rain fall in torrents, and to be sensible that Miss Miller had taken her place by my side. When I again unclosed my eyes, a loud bell was ringing; the girls were up and dressing; day had not yet begun to dawn, and a rushlight or two burned in the room. I too rose reluctantly; it was bitter cold, and I dressed as well as I could for shivering, and washed when there was a basin at liberty, which did not occur soon, as there was but one basin to six girls, on the stands down the middle of the room. Again the bell rang: all formed in file, two and two, and in that order descended the stairs and entered the cold and dimly lit schoolroom: here prayers were read by Miss Miller; afterwards she called out—

"Form classes!"

A great tumult succeeded for some minutes, during which Miss Miller repeatedly exclaimed, "Silence!" and

"Order!" When it subsided, I saw them all drawn up in four semicircles, before four chairs, placed at the four tables; all held books in their hands, and a great book, like a Bible, lay on each table, before the vacant seat. A pause of some seconds succeeded, filled up by the low, vague hum of numbers; Miss Miller walked from class to class, hushing this indefinite sound.

A distant bell tinkled: immediately three ladies entered the room, each walked to a table and took her seat; Miss Miller assumed the fourth vacant chair, which was that nearest the door, and around which the smallest of the children were assembled: to this inferior class I was called, and placed at the bottom of it.

Business now began: the day's Collect was repeated, then certain texts of Scripture were said, and to these succeeded a protracted reading of chapters in the Bible, which lasted an hour. By the time that exercise was terminated, day had fully dawned. The indefatigable bell now sounded for the fourth time: the classes were marshalled and marched into another room to breakfast: how glad I was to behold a prospect of getting something to eat! I was now nearly sick from inanition, having taken so little the day before.

The refectory was a great, low-ceiled, gloomy room; on two long tables smoked basins of something hot, which, however, to my dismay, sent forth an odour far from inviting. I saw a universal manifestation of discontent when the fumes of the repast met the nostrils of those destined to swallow it; from the van of the procession, the tall girls of the first class, rose the whispered words—

"Disgusting! The porridge is burnt again!"

"Silence!" ejaculated a voice; not that of Miss Miller, but one of the upper teachers, a little and dark personage, smartly dressed, but of somewhat morose aspect, who installed herself at the top of one table, while a more buxom lady presided at the other. I looked in vain for

her I had first seen the night before; she was not visible:
Miss Miller occupied the foot of the table where I sat,
and a strange, foreign-looking, elderly lady, the French
teacher, as I afterwards found, took the corresponding
seat at the other board. A long grace was said and a
hymn sung; then a servant brought in some tea for the
teachers, and the meal began.

Ravenous, and now very faint, I devoured a spoonful
or two of my portion without thinking of its taste; but
the first edge of hunger blunted, I perceived I had got in
hand a nauseous mess; burnt porridge is almost as bad
as rotten potatoes; famine itself soon sickens over it.
The spoons were moved slowly: I saw each girl taste her
food and try to swallow it; but in most cases the effort
was soon relinquished. Breakfast was over, and none
had breakfasted. Thanks being returned for what we
had not got, and a second hymn chanted, the refectory
was evacuated for the schoolroom. I was one of the last
to go out, and in passing the tables, I saw one teacher
take a basin of the porridge and taste it; she looked at
the others; all their countenances expressed displeasure,
and one of them, the stout one, whispered—

"Abominable stuff! How shameful!"

A quarter of an hour passed before lessons again began,
during which the schoolroom was in a glorious tumult;
for that space of time it seemed to be permitted to talk
loud and more freely, and they used their privilege. The
whole conversation ran on the breakfast, which one and
all abused roundly. Poor things! it was the sole con-
solation they had. Miss Miller was now the only teacher
in the room: a group of great girls standing about her
spoke with serious and sullen gestures. I heard the name
of Mr Brocklehurst pronounced by some lips; at which
Miss Miller shook her head disapprovingly; but she made
no great effort to check the general wrath; doubtless she
shared in it.

A clock in the schoolroom struck nine; Miss Miller

left her circle, and standing in the middle of the room, cried—

"Silence! To your seats!"

Discipline prevailed: in five minutes the confused throng was resolved into order, and comparative silence quelled the Babel clamour of tongues. The upper teachers now punctually resumed their posts: but still, all seemed to wait. Ranged on benches down the sides of the room, the eighty girls sat motionless and erect; a quaint assemblage they appeared, all with plain locks combed from their faces, not a curl visible; in brown dresses, made high and surrounded by a narrow tucker about the throat, with little pockets of holland (shaped something like a Highlander's purse) tied in front of their frocks, and destined to serve the purpose of a work-bag: all, too, wearing woollen stockings and country-made shoes, fastened with brass buckles. Above twenty of those clad in this costume were full-grown girls, or rather young women; it suited them ill, and gave an air of oddity even to the prettiest.

I was still looking at them, and also at intervals examining the teachers—none of whom precisely pleased me; for the stout one was a little coarse, the dark one not a little fierce, the foreigner harsh and grotesque, and Miss Miller, poor thing! looked purple, weather-beaten, and over-worked—when, as my eye wandered from face to face, the whole school rose simultaneously, as if moved by a common spring.

What was the matter? I had heard no order given: I was puzzled. Ere I had gathered my wits, the classes were again seated: but as all eyes were now turned to one point, mine followed the general direction, and encountered the personage who had received me last night. She stood at the bottom of the long room, on the hearth; for there was a fire at each end; she surveyed the two rows of girls silently and gravely. Miss Miller approaching, seemed to ask her a question, and having received her answer, went back to her place, and said aloud—

"Monitor of the first class, fetch the globes!"

While the direction was being executed, the lady consulted moved slowly up the room. I suppose I have a considerable organ of veneration, for I retain yet the sense of admiring awe with which my eyes traced her steps. Seen now, in broad daylight, she looked tall, fair, and shapely; brown eyes with a benignant light in their irises, and a fine pencilling of long lashes round, relieved the whiteness of her large front; on each of her temples her hair, of a very dark brown, was clustered in round curls, according to the fashion of those times, when neither smooth bands nor long ringlets were in vogue; her dress, also in the mode of the day, was of purple cloth, relieved by a sort of Spanish trimming of black velvet; a gold watch (watches were not so common then as now) shone at her girdle. Let the reader add, to complete the picture, refined features; a complexion, if pale, clear; and a stately air and carriage, and he will have, at least as clearly as words can give it, a correct idea of the exterior of Miss Temple—Maria Temple, as I afterwards saw the name written in a prayer-book intrusted to me to carry to church.

The superintendent of Lowood (for such was this lady) having taken her seat before a pair of globes placed on one of the tables, summoned the first class round her, and commenced giving a lesson on geography; the lower classes were called by the teachers: repetitions in history, grammar, etc., went on for an hour; writing and arithmetic succeeded, and music lessons were given by Miss Temple to some of the elder girls. The duration of each lesson was measured by the clock, which at last struck twelve. The superintendent rose—

"I have a word to address to the pupils," said she.

The tumult of cessation from lessons was already breaking forth, but it sank at her voice. She went on—

"You had this morning a breakfast which you could not eat; you must be hungry:—I have ordered that a lunch of bread and cheese shall be served to all."

The teachers looked at her with a sort of surprise.

"It is to be done on my responsibility," she added, in an explanatory tone to them, and immediately afterwards left the room.

The bread and cheese was presently brought in and distributed, to the high delight and refreshment of the whole school. The order was now given "To the garden!" Each put on a coarse straw bonnet, with strings of coloured calico, and a cloak of grey frieze. I was similarly equipped, and, following the stream, I made my way into the open air.

The garden was a wide inclosure, surrounded with walls so high as to exclude every glimpse of prospect; a covered verandah ran down one side, and broad walks bordered a middle space divided into scores of little beds: these beds were assigned as gardens for the pupils to cultivate, and each bed had an owner. When full of flowers they would doubtless look pretty; but now, at the latter end of January, all was wintry blight and brown decay. I shuddered as I stood and looked round me: it was an inclement day for outdoor exercise; not positively rainy, but darkened by a drizzling yellow fog; all under foot was still soaking wet with the floods of yesterday. The stronger among the girls ran about and engaged in active games, but sundry pale and thin ones herded together for shelter and warmth in the verandah; and amongst these, as the dense mist penetrated to their shivering frames, I heard frequently the sound of a hollow cough.

As yet I had spoken to no one, nor did anybody seem to take notice of me; I stood lonely enough: but to that feeling of isolation I was accustomed; it did not oppress me much. I leant against a pillar of the verandah, drew my grey mantle close about me, and, trying to forget the cold which nipped me without, and the unsatisfied hunger which gnawed me within, delivered myself up to the employment of watching and thinking. My reflections were too undefined and fragmentary to merit record: I hardly yet knew where I was; Gateshead and my past life seemed floated away to an immeasurable distance; the present was vague and strange, and of the future I could form no conjecture. I looked round the convent-like garden, and then up at the house—a large building, half of which seemed grey and old, the other half quite new. The new part, containing the schoolroom and dormitory, was lit by mullioned and latticed windows, which gave it a church-like aspect; a stone tablet over the door bore this inscription:

"Lowood Institution.—This portion was rebuilt A.D. ——, by Naomi Brocklehurst, of Brocklehurst Hall, in this county." "Let your light so shine before men, that they may see your good works, and glorify your Father which is in heaven."—St Matt. v. 16.

I read these words over and over again: I felt that an explanation belonged to them, and was unable fully to penetrate their import. I was still pondering the signification of "Institution," and endeavouring to make out a connection between the first words and the verse of Scripture, when the sound of a cough close behind me made me turn my head. I saw a girl sitting on a stone bench near; she was bent over a book, on the perusal of which she seemed intent: from where I stood I could see the title—it was *Rasselas*; a name that struck me as strange, and consequently attractive. In turning a leaf she happened to look up, and I said to her directly—

"Is your book interesting?" I had already formed the intention of asking her to lend it to me some day.

"I like it," she answered, after a pause of a second or two, during which she examined me.

"What is it about?" I continued. I hardly know where I found the hardihood thus to open a conversation with a stranger; the step was contrary to my nature and habits:

but I think her occupation touched a chord of sympathy somewhere; for I too liked reading, though of a frivolous and childish kind; I could not digest or comprehend the serious or substantial.

"You may look at it," replied the girl, offering me the book.

I did so; a brief examination convinced me that the contents were less taking than the title: *Rasselas* looked dull to my trifling taste; I saw nothing about fairies, nothing about genii; no bright variety seemed spread over the closely-printed pages. I returned it to her; she received it quietly, and without saying anything she was about to relapse into her former studious mood: again I ventured to disturb her—

"Can you tell me what the writing on that stone over the door means? What is Lowood Institution?"

"This house where you are come to live."

"And why do they call it Institution? Is it in any way different from other schools?"

"It is partly a charity-school: you and I, and all the rest of us, are charity-children. I suppose you are an orphan: are not either your father or your mother dead?"

"Both died before I can remember."

"Well, all the girls here have lost either one or both parents, and this is called an institution for educating orphans."

"Do we pay no money? Do they keep us for nothing?"

"We pay, or our friends pay, fifteen pounds a year for each."

"Then why do they call us charity-children?"

"Because fifteen pounds is not enough for board and teaching, and the deficiency is supplied by subscription."

"Who subscribes?"

"Different benevolent-minded ladies and gentlemen in this neighbourhood and in London."

"Who was Naomi Brocklehurst?"

"The lady who built the new part of this house as that

tablet records, and whose son overlooks and directs everything here."

"Why?"

"Because he is treasurer and manager of the establishment."

"Then this house does not belong to that tall lady who wears a watch, and who said we were to have some bread and cheese?"

"To Miss Temple? Oh, no! I wish it did: she has to answer to Mr Brocklehurst for all she does. Mr Brocklehurst buys all our food and all our clothes."

"Does he live here?"

"No—two miles off, at a large hall."

"Is he a good man?"

"He is a clergyman, and is said to do a great deal of good."

"Did you say that tall lady was called Miss Temple?"

"Yes."

"And what are the other teachers called?"

"The one with red cheeks is called Miss Smith; she attends to the work, and cuts out—for we make our own clothes, our frocks, and pelisses, and everything; the little one with black hair is Miss Scatcherd; she teaches history and grammar, and hears the second class repetitions; and the one who wears a shawl, and has a pocket-handkerchief tied to her side with a yellow ribband, is Madame Pierrot: she comes from Lisle, in France, and teaches French."

"Do you like the teachers?"

"Well enough."

"Do you like the little black one, and the Madame ——?—I cannot pronounce her name as you do."

"Miss Scatcherd is hasty—you must take care not to offend her; Madame Pierrot is not a bad sort of person."

"But Miss Temple is the best—isn't she?"

"Miss Temple is very good and very clever; she is above the rest, because she knows far more than they do."

"Have you been long here?"

"Two years."

"Are you an orphan?"

"My mother is dead."

"Are you happy here?"

"You ask rather too many questions. I have given you answers enough for the present: now I want to read."

But at that moment the summons sounded for dinner; all re-entered the house. The odour which now filled the refectory was scarcely more appetising than that which had regaled our nostrils at breakfast: the dinner was served in two huge tin-plated vessels, whence rose a strong steam redolent of rancid fat. I found the mess to consist of indifferent potatoes and strange shreds of rusty meat, mixed and cooked together. Of this preparation a tolerably abundant plateful was apportioned to each pupil. I ate what I could, and wondered within myself whether every day's fare would be like this.

After dinner, we immediately adjourned to the schoolroom: lessons recommenced, and were continued till five o'clock.

The only marked event of the afternoon was, that I saw the girl with whom I had conversed in the verandah dismissed in disgrace by Miss Scatcherd from a history class, and sent to stand in the middle of the large schoolroom. The punishment seemed to me in a high degree ignominious, especially for so great a girl—she looked thirteen or upwards. I expected she would show signs of great distress and shame; but to my surprise she neither wept nor blushed: composed, though grave, she stood, the central mark of all eyes. "How can she bear it so quietly—so firmly?" I asked of myself. "Were I in her place, it seems to me I should wish the earth to open and swallow me up. She looks as if she were thinking of something beyond her punishment—beyond her situation: of something not round her. nor before her. I have heard of day-dreams—is she in a day-dream now? Her eyes are fixed on the floor, but I am sure they do not see it—her sight seems turned in, gone down into her heart: she is looking at what she can remember, I believe; not at what is really present. I wonder what sort of a girl she is—whether good or naughty."

Soon after five p.m. we had another meal, consisting of a small mug of coffee, and half a slice of brown bread. I devoured my bread and drank my coffee with relish; but I should have been glad of as much more—I was still hungry. Half an hour's recreation succeeded, then study; then the glass of water and the piece of oat-cake, prayers, and bed. Such was my first day at Lowood.

MR ROCHESTER

from *Jane Eyre*.

THE promise of a smooth career, which my first calm introduction to Thornfield Hall seemed to pledge, was not belied on a longer acquaintance with the place and its inmates. Mrs Fairfax turned out to be what she appeared, a placid-tempered, kind-natured woman, of competent education and average intelligence. My pupil was a lively child, who had been spoilt and indulged, and therefore was sometimes wayward; but as she was committed entirely to my care, and no injudicious inter-ference from any quarter ever thwarted my plans for her improvement, she soon forgot her little freaks, and became obedient and teachable. She had no great talents, no marked traits of character, no peculiar development of feeling or taste which raised her one inch above the ordinary level of childhood; but neither had she any deficiency or vice which sunk her below it. She made reasonable progress, entertained for me a vivacious, though perhaps not very profound, affection; and by her simplicity, gay prattle, and efforts to please, inspired me, in return, with a degree of attachment sufficient to make us both content in each other's society.

This, *par parenthèse*, will be thought cool language by persons who entertain solemn doctrines about the angelic nature of children, and the duty of those charged with their education to conceive for them an idolatrous devotion: but I am not writing to flatter parental egotism, to echo cant, or prop up humbug; I am merely telling the truth. I felt a conscientious solicitude for Adèle's welfare and progress, and a quiet liking for her little self: just as I cherished towards Mrs Fairfax a thankfulness for her kindness, and a pleasure in her society proportionate to the tranquil regard she had for me, and the moderation of her mind and character.

Anybody may blame me who likes, when I add further, that, now and then, when I took a walk by myself in the grounds; when I went down to the gates and looked through them along the road; or when, while Adèle played with her nurse, and Mrs Fairfax made jellies in the storeroom, I climbed the three staircases, raised the trap-door of the attic, and having reached the leads, looked out afar over sequestered field and hill, and along dim sky-line—that then I longed for a power of vision which might overpass that limit; which might reach the busy world, towns, regions full of life I had heard of but never seen—that then I desired more of practical experience than I possessed; more of intercourse with my kind, of acquaintance with variety of character, than was here within my reach. I valued what was good in Mrs Fairfax, and what was good in Adèle; but I believed in the existence of other and more vivid kinds of goodness, and what I believed in I wished to behold.

Who blames me? Many, no doubt; and I shall be called discontented. I could not help it; the restlessness was in my nature; it agitated me to pain sometimes. Then my sole relief was to walk along the corridor of the third storey, backwards and forwards, safe in the silence and solitude of the spot, and allow my mind's eye to dwell on whatever bright visions rose before it—and, certainly, they were many and glowing; to let my heart be heaved by the exultant movement, which, while it swelled it in trouble, expanded it with life; and, best of all, to open my inward ear to a tale that was never ended —a tale my imagination created, and narrated continuously; quickened with all of incident, life, fire, feeling, that I desired and had not in my actual existence.

It is in vain to say human beings ought to be satisfied with tranquillity: they must have action; and they will make it if they cannot find it. Millions are condemned to a stiller doom than mine, and millions are in silent revolt against their lot. Nobody knows how many rebellions besides political rebellions ferment in the masses of life which people earth. Women are supposed to be very calm generally: but women feel just as men feel; they need exercise for their faculties, and a field for their efforts, as much as their brothers do; they suffer from too rigid a restraint, too absolute a stagnation, precisely as men would suffer; and it is narrow-minded in their more privileged fellow-creatures to say that they ought to confine themselves to making puddings and knitting stockings, to playing on the piano and embroidering bags. It is thoughtless to condemn them, or laugh at them, if they seek to do more or learn more than custom has pronounced necessary for their sex. . . .

October, November, December passed away. One afternoon in January, Mrs Fairfax had begged a holiday for Adèle, because she had a cold; and, as Adèle seconded the request with an ardour that reminded me how precious occasional holidays had been to me in my own childhood, I accorded it, deeming that I did well in showing pliability on the point. It was a fine, calm day, though very cold; I was tired of sitting still in the library through a whole long morning: Mrs Fairfax had just written a letter which was waiting to be posted, so I put on my bonnet and cloak and volunteered to carry it to Hay; the distance, two miles, would be a pleasant winter afternoon walk. Having seen Adèle comfortably seated in her little chair by Mrs Fairfax's parlour fireside, and given her her best wax doll (which I usually kept enveloped in silver paper in a drawer) to play with, and a story-book for change of amusement; and having replied to her "Revenez bientôt, ma bonne amie, ma chère Mdlle. Jeannette," with a kiss I set out.

The ground was hard, the air was still, my road was lonely; I walked fast till I got warm, and then I walked slowly to enjoy and analyse the species of pleasure brooding for me in the hour and situation. It was three o'clock; the church bell tolled as I passed under the belfry: the charm of the hour lay in its approaching dimness, in the low-gliding and pale-beaming sun. I was a mile from Thornfield, in a lane noted for wild roses in summer, for nuts and blackberries in autumn, and even now possessing a few coral treasures in hips and haws, but whose best winter delight lay in its utter solitude and leafless repose. If a breath of air stirred, it made no sound here; for there was not a holly, not an evergreen to rustle, and the stripped hawthorn and hazel bushes were as still as the white, worn stones which causewayed the middle of the path. Far and wide, on each side, there were only fields, where no cattle now browsed; and the little brown birds, which stirred occasionally in the hedge, looked like single russet leaves that had forgotten to drop.

This lane inclined up-hill all the way to Hay; having reached the middle, I sat down on a stile which led thence into a field. Gathering my mantle about me, and sheltering my hands in my muff, I did not feel the cold, though it froze keenly; as was attested by a sheet of ice covering the causeway, where a little brooklet, now congealed, had overflowed after a rapid thaw some days since. From my seat I could look down on Thornfield: the grey and battlemented hall was the principal object in the vale below me; its woods and dark rookery rose against the west. I lingered till the sun went down amongst the trees, and sank crimson and clear behind them. I then turned eastward.

On the hill-top above me sat the rising moon; pale yet as a cloud, but brightening momentarily, she looked over Hay, which, half lost in trees, sent up a blue smoke from its few chimneys: it was yet a mile distant, but in the absolute hush I could hear plainly its thin murmurs of life. My ear, too, felt the flow of currents; in what dales and depths I could not tell: but there were many hills beyond Hay, and doubtless many becks threading their passes. That evening calm betrayed alike the tinkle of the nearest streams, the sough of the most remote.

A rude noise broke on these fine ripplings and whisperings, at once so far away and so clear: a positive tramp, tramp, a metallic clatter, which effaced the soft wave-wanderings; as, in a picture, the solid mass of a crag, or the rough boles of a great oak, drawn in dark and strong on the foreground, efface the aërial distance of azure hill, sunny horizon, and blended clouds where tint melts into tint.

The din was on the causeway: a horse was coming; the windings of the lane yet hid it, but it approached. I was just leaving the stile; yet, as the path was narrow, I sat still to let it go by. In those days I was young, and all sorts of fancies bright and dark tenanted my mind: the memories of nursery stories were there amongst other rubbish; and when they recurred, maturing youth added to them a vigour and vividness beyond what childhood could give. As this horse approached, and as I watched for it to appear through the dusk, I remembered certain of Bessie's tales, wherein figured a North-of-England spirit called a "Gytrash," which, in the form of horse, mule, or large dog, haunted solitary ways, and sometimes came upon belated travellers, as this horse was now coming upon me.

It was very near, but not yet in sight; when, in addition to the tramp, tramp, I heard a rush under the hedge, and close down by the hazel stems glided a great dog, whose black and white colour made him a distinct object against the trees. It was exactly one form of Bessie's Gytrash—a lion-like creature with long hair and a huge head: it passed me, however, quietly enough, not staying to look up, with strange pretercanine eyes, in my face, as I half expected it would. The horse followed,—a tall steed, and on its back a rider. The man, the human being, broke the spell at once. Nothing ever rode the Gytrash: it was always alone; and goblins, to my notions, though they might tenant the dumb carcasses of beasts, could scarce covet shelter in the commonplace human form. No Gytrash was this,—only a traveller taking the short cut to Millcote. He passed, and I went on; a few steps, and I turned: a sliding sound and an exclamation of "What the deuce is to do now?" and a clattering tumble, arrested my attention. Man and horse were down; they had slipped on the sheet of ice which glazed the causeway. The dog came bounding back, and seeing his master in a predicament, and hearing the horse groan, barked till the evening hills echoed the sound, which was deep in proportion to his magnitude. He snuffed round the prostrate group, and then he ran up to me; it was all he could do,—there was no other help at hand to summon. I obeyed him, and walked down to the traveller, by this time struggling himself free of his steed. His efforts were so vigorous, I thought he could not be much hurt; but I asked him the question—

"Are you injured, sir?"

I think he was swearing, but am not certain; however, he was pronouncing some formula which prevented him from replying to me directly.

"Can I do anything?" I asked again.

"You must just stand on one side," he answered as he rose, first to his knees, and then to his feet. I did;

whereupon began a heaving, stamping, clattering process, accompanied by a barking and baying which removed me effectually some yards' distance; but I would not be driven quite away till I saw the event. This was finally fortunate; the horse was re-established, and the dog was silenced with a "Down, Pilot!" The traveller now, stooping, felt his foot and leg, as if trying whether they were sound; apparently something ailed them, for he halted to the stile whence I had just risen, and sat down.

I was in the mood for being useful, or at least officious, I think, for I now drew near him again.

"If you are hurt, and want help, sir, I can fetch some one either from Thornfield Hall or from Hay."

"Thank you: I shall do: I have no broken bones,— only a sprain"; and again he stood up and tried his foot, but the result extorted an involuntary "Ugh!"

Something of daylight still lingered, and the moon was waxing bright: I could see him plainly. His figure was enveloped in a riding cloak, fur collared and steel clasped; its details were not apparent, but I traced the general points of middle height and considerable breadth of chest. He had a dark face, with stern features and a heavy brow; his eyes and gathered eyebrows looked ireful and thwarted just now; he was past youth, but had not reached middle-age; perhaps he might be thirty-five. I felt no fear of him, and but little shyness. Had he been a handsome, heroic-looking young gentleman, I should not have dared to stand thus questioning him against his will, and offering my services unasked. I had hardly ever seen a handsome youth; never in my life spoken to one. I had a theoretical reverence and homage for beauty, elegance, gallantry, fascination; but had I met those qualities incarnate in masculine shape, I should have known instinctively that they neither had nor could have sympathy with anything in me, and should have shunned them as one would fire, lightning, or anything else that is bright but antipathetic.

If even this stranger had smiled and been good-humoured to me when I addressed him; if he had put off my offer of assistance gaily and with thanks, I should have gone on my way and not felt any vocation to renew inquiries: but the frown, the roughness of the traveller, set me at my ease: I retained my station when he waved to me to go, and announced—

"I cannot think of leaving you, sir, at so late an hour, in this solitary lane, till I see you are fit to mount your horse."

He looked at me when I said this; he had hardly turned his eyes in my direction before.

"I should think you ought to be at home yourself," said he, "if you have a home in this neighbourhood: where do you come from?"

"From just below; and I am not at all afraid of being out late when it is moonlight: I will run over to Hay for you with pleasure, if you wish it: indeed, I am going there to post a letter."

"You live just below—do you mean at that house with the battlements?" pointing to Thornfield Hall, on which the moon cast a hoary gleam, bringing it out distinct and pale from the woods, that, by contrast with the western sky, now seemed one mass of shadow.

"Yes, sir."

"Whose house is it?"

"Mr Rochester's."

"Do you know Mr Rochester?"

"No, I have never seen him."

"He is not resident, then?"

"No."

"Can you tell me where he is?"

"I cannot."

"You are not a servant at the hall, of course. You are——" He stopped, ran his eye over my dress, which, as usual, was quite simple: a black merino cloak, a black beaver bonnet; neither of them half fine enough for a

lady's-maid. He seemed puzzled to decide what I was;
I helped him.

"I am the governess."

"Ah, the governess!" he repeated; "deuce take me,
if I had not forgotten! The governess!" and again my
raiment underwent scrutiny. In two minutes he rose from
the stile: his face expressed pain when he tried to move.

"I cannot commission you to fetch help," he said;
"but you may help me a little yourself, if you will be so
kind."

"Yes, sir."

"You have not an umbrella that I can use as a stick?"

"No."

"Try to get hold of my horse's bridle and lead him to
me: you are not afraid?"

I should have been afraid to touch a horse when alone,
but when told to do it, I was disposed to obey. I put
down my muff on the stile, and went up to the tall steed;
I endeavoured to catch the bridle, but it was a spirited
thing, and would not let me come near its head; I
made effort on effort, though in vain: meantime, I was
mortally afraid of its trampling fore-feet. The traveller
waited and watched for some time, and at last he
laughed.

"I see," he said, "the mountain will never be brought
to Mahomet, so all you can do is to aid Mahomet to go
to the mountain; I must beg of you to come here."

I came. "Excuse me," he continued: "necessity
compels me to make you useful." He laid a heavy hand
on my shoulder, and leaning on me with some stress,
limped to his horse. Having once caught the bridle, he
mastered it directly and sprang to his saddle; grimacing
grimly as he made the effort, for it wrenched his sprain.

"Now," said he, releasing his under lip from a hard
bite, "just hand me my whip; it lies there under the
hedge."

I sought it and found it.

"Thank you; now make haste with the letter to Hay, and return as fast as you can."

A touch of a spurred heel made his horse first start and rear, and then bound away; the dog rushed in his traces; all three vanished,

> Like heath that, in the wilderness,
> The wild wind whirls away.

I took up my muff and walked on. The incident had occurred and was gone for me: it *was* an incident of no moment, no romance, no interest in a sense; yet it marked with change one single hour of a monotonous life. My help had been needed and claimed; I had given it: I was pleased to have done something; trivial, transitory though the deed was, it was yet an active thing, and I was weary of an existence all passive. The new face, too, was like a new picture introduced to the gallery of memory; and it was dissimilar to all the others hanging there: firstly, because it was masculine; and, secondly, because it was dark, strong, and stern. I had it still before me when I entered Hay, and slipped the letter into the post-office; I saw it as I walked fast down-hill all the way home. When I came to the stile, I stopped a minute, looked round and listened, with an idea that a horse's hoofs might ring on the causeway again, and that a rider in a cloak, and a Gytrash-like Newfoundland dog, might be again apparent: I saw only the hedge and a pollard willow before me, rising up still and straight to meet the moonbeams; I heard only the faintest waft of wind roaming fitful among the trees round Thornfield, a mile distant; and when I glanced down in the direction of the murmur, my eye, traversing the hall-front, caught a light kindling in a window: it reminded me that I was late, and I hurried on.

I did not like re-entering Thornfield. To pass its threshold was to return to stagnation; to cross the silent hall, to ascend the darksome staircase, to seek my own lonely little room, and then to meet tranquil Mrs Fairfax, and spend the long winter evening with her, and her only, was to quell wholly the faint excitement wakened by my walk,—to slip again over my faculties the viewless fetters of an uniform and too still existence; of an existence whose very privileges of security and ease I was becoming incapable of appreciating. What good it would have done me at that time to have been tossed in the storms of an uncertain struggling life, and to have been taught by rough and bitter experience to long for the calm amidst which I now repined! Yes, just as much good as it would do a man tired of sitting still in a "too easy chair" to take a long walk: and just as natural was the wish to stir, under my circumstances, as it would be under his.

I lingered at the gates; I lingered on the lawn; I paced backwards and forwards on the pavement; the shutters of the glass door were closed; I could not see into the interior; and both my eyes and spirit seemed drawn from the gloomy house—from the grey hollow filled with rayless cells, as it appeared to me—to that sky expanded before me,—a blue sea absolved from taint of cloud; the moon ascending it in solemn march; her orb seeming to look up as she left the hill-tops, from behind which she had come, far and farther below her, and aspired to the zenith, midnight dark in its fathomless depth and measureless distance; and for those trembling stars that followed her course; they made my heart tremble, my veins glow when I viewed them. Little things recall us to earth; the clock struck in the hall; that sufficed; I turned from moon and stars, opened a side-door, and went in.

The hall was not dark, nor yet was it lit, only by the high-hung bronze lamp; a warm glow suffused both it and the lower steps of the oak staircase. This ruddy shine issued from the great dining-room, whose two-leaved door stood open, and showed a genial fire in the grate, glancing on marble hearth and brass fire-irons, and revealing purple draperies and polished furniture, in the most pleasant radiance. It revealed, too, a group near the mantelpiece: I had scarcely caught it, and scarcely become aware of a cheerful mingling of voices, amongst which I seemed to distinguish the tones of Adèle, when the door closed.

I hastened to Mrs Fairfax's room; there was a fire there too, but no candle, and no Mrs Fairfax. Instead, all alone, sitting upright on the rug, and gazing with gravity at the blaze, I beheld a great black and white long-haired dog, just like the Gytrash of the lane. It was so like it that I went forward and said—"Pilot," and the thing got up and came to me and snuffed me. I caressed him, and he wagged his great tail; but he looked an eerie creature to be alone with, and I could not tell whence he had come. I rang the bell, for I wanted a candle; and I wanted, too, to get an account of this visitant. Leah entered.

"What dog is this?"

"He came with master."

"With whom?"

"With master—Mr Rochester—he is just arrived."

"Indeed! and is Mrs Fairfax with him?"

"Yes, and Miss Adèle; they are in the dining-room, and John is gone for a surgeon; for master has had an accident; his horse fell and his ankle is sprained."

"Did the horse fall in Hay Lane?"

"Yes, coming down-hill; it slipped on some ice."

"Ah! Bring me a candle, will you, Leah?"

Leah brought it; she entered, followed by Mrs Fairfax, who repeated the news; adding that Mr Carter the surgeon was come, and was now with Mr Rochester: then she hurried out to give orders about tea, and I went upstairs to take off my things.

THE INTERRUPTED WEDDING

from *Jane Eyre*.

SOPHIE came at seven to dress me: she was very long indeed in accomplishing her task; so long that Mr Rochester, grown, I suppose, impatient of my delay, sent up to ask why I did not come. She was just fastening my veil (the plain square of blond after all) to my hair with a brooch; I hurried from under her hands as soon as I could.

"Stop!" she cried in French. "Look at yourself in the mirror: you have not taken one peep."

So I turned at the door: I saw a robed and veiled figure, so unlike my usual self that it seemed almost the image of a stranger. "Jane!" called a voice, and I hastened down. I was received at the foot of the stairs by Mr Rochester.

"Lingerer!" he said, "my brain is on fire with impatience, and you tarry so long!"

He took me into the dining-room, surveyed me keenly all over, pronounced me "fair as a lily, and not only the pride of his life, but the desire of his eyes," and then telling me he would give me but ten minutes to eat some breakfast, he rang the bell. One of his lately hired servants, a footman, answered it.

"Is John getting the carriage ready?"

"Yes, sir."

"Is the luggage brought down?"

"They are bringing it down, sir."

"Go you to the church: see if Mr Wood (the clergyman) and the clerk are there: return and tell me."

The church, as the reader knows, was but just beyond the gates; the footman soon returned.

"Mr Wood is in the vestry, sir, putting on his surplice."

"And the carriage?"

"The horses are harnessing."

"We shall not want it to go to church; but it must be ready the moment we return: all the boxes and luggage arranged and strapped on, and the coachman in his seat."

"Yes, sir."

"Jane, are you ready?"

I rose. There were no groomsmen, no bridesmaids, no relatives to wait for or marshal: none but Mr Rochester and I. Mrs Fairfax stood in the hall as we passed. I would fain have spoken to her, but my hand was held by a grasp of iron: I was hurried along by a stride I could hardly follow; and to look at Mr Rochester's face was to feel that not a second of delay would be tolerated for any purpose. I wonder what other bridegroom ever looked as he did—so bent up to a purpose, so grimly resolute: or who, under such steadfast brows, ever revealed such flaming and flashing eyes.

I know not whether the day was fair or foul; in descending the drive, I gazed neither on sky nor earth: my heart was with my eyes; and both seemed migrated into Mr Rochester's frame. I wanted to see the invisible thing on which, as we went along, he appeared to fasten a glance fierce and fell. I wanted to feel the thoughts whose force he seemed breasting and resisting.

At the churchyard wicket he stopped: he discovered I was quite out of breath. "Am I cruel in my love?" he said. "Delay an instant: lean on me, Jane."

And now I can recall the picture of the grey old house of God rising calm before me, of a rook wheeling round the steeple, of a ruddy morning sky beyond. I remember something, too, of the green grave-moulds; and I have not forgotten, either, two figures of strangers straying amongst the low hillocks and reading the mementoes graven on the few mossy head-stones. I noticed them, because, as they saw us, they passed round to the back of the church; and I doubted not they were going to enter by the side-aisle door and witness the ceremony. By Mr Rochester they were not observed; he was earnestly looking at my face, from which the blood had, I daresay, momentarily fled: for I felt my forehead dewy, and my cheeks and lips cold. When I rallied, which I soon did, he walked gently with me up the path to the porch.

We entered the quiet and humble temple; the priest waited in his white surplice at the lowly altar, the clerk beside him. All was still: two shadows only moved in a remote corner. My conjecture had been correct: the strangers had slipped in before us, and they now stood by the vault of the Rochesters, their backs towards us, viewing through the rails the old time-stained marble tomb, where a kneeling angel guarded the remains of Damer de Rochester, slain at Marston Moor in the time of the civil wars, and of Elizabeth, his wife.

Our place was taken at the communion rails. Hearing a cautious step behind me, I glanced over my shoulder: one of the strangers—a gentleman, evidently—was advancing up the chancel. The service began. The explanation of the intent of matrimony was gone through; and then the clergyman came a step farther forward, and, bending slightly towards Mr Rochester, went on:

"I require and charge you both (as ye will answer at the dreadful day of judgment, when the secrets of all hearts shall be disclosed), that if either of you know any impediment why ye may not lawfully be joined together in matrimony, ye do now confess it; for be ye well assured that so many as are coupled together otherwise than God's Word doth allow, are not joined together by God, neither is their matrimony lawful."

He paused, as the custom is. When is the pause after that sentence ever broken by reply? Not, perhaps, once in a hundred years. And the clergyman, who had not lifted his eyes from his book, and had held his breath but for a moment, was proceeding: his hand was already stretched towards Mr Rochester, as his lips unclosed to ask, "Wilt thou have this woman for thy wedded wife?" —when a distinct and near voice said—

"The marriage cannot go on: I declare the existence of an impediment."

The clergyman looked up at the speaker and stood mute; the clerk did the same; Mr Rochester moved slightly, as if an earthquake had rolled under his feet: taking a firmer footing, and not turning his head or eyes, he said, "Proceed."

Profound silence fell when he had uttered that word, with deep but low intonation. Presently Mr Wood said—

"I cannot proceed without some investigation into what has been asserted, and evidence of its truth or falsehood."

"The ceremony is quite broken off," subjoined the voice behind us. "I am in a condition to prove my allegation: an insuperable impediment to this marriage exists."

Mr Rochester heard, but heeded not: he stood stubborn and rigid, making no movement but to possess himself of my hand. What a hot and strong grasp he had! and how like quarried marble was his pale, firm, massive front at this moment! How his eye shone, still watchful, and yet wild beneath!

Mr Wood seemed at a loss. "What is the nature of the impediment?" he asked. "Perhaps it may be got over—explained away?"

"Hardly," was the answer. "I have called it insuperable, and I speak advisedly."

The speaker came forward and leaned on the rails. He continued, uttering each word distinctly, calmly, steadily, but not loudly—

"It simply consists in the existence of a previous marriage. Mr Rochester has a wife now living." . . .

That night I never thought to sleep; but a slumber fell on me as soon as I lay down in bed. I was transported in thought to the scenes of childhood: I dreamt I lay in the red-room at Gateshead; that the night was dark, and my mind impressed with strange fears. The light that long ago had struck me into syncope, recalled in this vision, seemed glidingly to mount the wall, and tremblingly to pause in the centre of the obscured ceiling. I lifted up my head to look: the roof resolved to clouds, high and dim; the gleam was such as the moon imparts to vapours she is about to sever. I watched her come—watched with the strangest anticipation; as though some word of doom were to be written on her disk. She broke forth as never moon yet burst from cloud: a hand first penetrated the sable folds and waved them away; then, not a moon, but a white human form shone in the azure, inclining a glorious brow earthward. It gazed and gazed on me. It spoke to my spirit: immeasurably distant was the tone, yet so near, it whispered in my heart—

"My daughter, flee temptation."

"Mother, I will."

So I answered after I had waked from the trance-like dream. It was yet night, but July nights are short: soon after midnight, dawn comes. "It cannot be too early to commence the task I have to fulfil," thought I. I rose: I was dressed; for I had taken off nothing but my shoes. I knew where to find in my drawers some linen, a locket, a ring. In seeking these articles, I encountered the beads of a pearl necklace Mr Rochester had forced me to accept a few days ago. I left that; it was not mine: it was the visionary bride's who had melted in air. The other articles I made up in a parcel; my purse, containing twenty shillings (it was all I had), I put in my pocket: I tied on my straw bonnet, pinned my shawl, took the parcel and my slippers, which I would not put on yet, and stole from my room.

"Farewell, kind Mrs Fairfax!" I whispered, as I glided past her door. "Farewell, my darling Adèle!" I said, as I glanced towards the nursery. No thought could be admitted of entering to embrace her. I had to deceive a fine ear: for aught I knew it might now be listening.

I would have got past Mr Rochester's chamber without a pause; but my heart momentarily stopping its beat at that threshold, my foot was forced to stop also. No sleep was there: the inmate was walking restlessly from wall to wall; and again and again he sighed while I listened. There was a heaven—a temporary heaven—in this room for me, if I chose: I had but to go in and to say—

"Mr Rochester, I will love you and live with you through life till death," and a fount of rapture would spring to my lips. I thought of this.

That kind master, who could not sleep now, was waiting with impatience for day. He would send for me in the morning; I should be gone. He would have me sought for: vainly. He would feel himself forsaken; his love rejected: he would suffer; perhaps grow desperate. I thought of this too. My hand moved towards the lock: I caught it back, and glided on.

Drearily I wound my way downstairs: I knew what I had to do, and I did it mechanically. I sought the key of the side-door in the kitchen; I sought, too, a phial of oil and a feather; I oiled the key and the lock. I got some water, I got some bread: for perhaps I should have to walk far; and my strength, sorely shaken of late, must not break down. All this I did without one sound. I opened the door, passed out, shut it softly. Dim dawn glimmered in the yard. The great gates were closed and locked; but a wicket in one of them was only latched. Through that I departed: it, too, I shut; and now I was out of Thornfield.

A mile off, beyond the fields, lay a road which stretched in the contrary direction to Millcote; a road I had never travelled, but often noticed, and wondered where it led: thither I bent my steps. No reflection was to be allowed now: not one glance was to be cast back; not even one forward. Not one thought was to be given either to the past or the future. The first was a page so heavenly sweet—so deadly sad—that to read one line of it would dissolve my courage and break down my energy. The last was an awful blank: something like the world when the deluge was gone by.

I skirted fields, and hedges, and lanes till after sunrise. I believe it was a lovely summer morning: I know my shoes, which I had put on when I left the house, were soon wet with dew. But I looked neither to rising sun, nor smiling sky, nor wakening nature. . . .

Still I could not turn, nor retrace one step. God must have led me on. As to my own will or conscience, impassioned grief had trampled one and stifled the other. I was weeping wildly as I walked along my solitary way: fast, fast I went like one delirious. A weakness, beginning inwardly, extending to the limbs, seized me, and I fell: I lay on the ground some minutes, pressing my face to the wet turf. I had some fear—or hope—that here I should die: but I was soon up; crawling forwards on my hands and knees, and then again raised to my feet —as eager and as determined as ever to reach the road.

When I got there, I was forced to sit to rest me under the hedge; and while I sat, I heard wheels, and saw a coach come on. I stood up and lifted my hand; it stopped. I asked where it was going: the driver named a place a long way off, and where I was sure Mr Rochester had no connections. I asked for what sum he would take me there; he said thirty shillings; I answered I had but twenty; well, he would try to make it do. He further gave me leave to get into the inside, as the vehicle was empty: I entered, was shut in, and it rolled on its way.

Gentle reader, may you never feel what I then felt! May your eyes never shed such stormy, scalding, heart-wrung tears as poured from mine. May you never appeal to Heaven in prayers so hopeless and so agonised as in that hour left my lips; for never may you, like me, dread to be the instrument of evil to what you wholly love.

Two days are passed. It is a summer evening; the

coachman has set me down at a place called Whitcross;
he could take me no farther for the sum I had given, and
I was not possessed of another shilling in the world. The
coach is a mile off by this time; I am alone. At this
moment I discover that I forgot to take my parcel out
of the pocket of the coach, where I had placed it for
safety; there it remains, there it must remain; and now,
I am absolutely destitute.

Whitcross is no town, nor even a hamlet; it is but a
stone pillar set up where four roads meet: white-washed,
I suppose, to be more obvious at a distance and in darkness. Four arms spring from its summit: the nearest town
to which these point is, according to the inscription,
distant ten miles; the farthest, above twenty. From the
well-known names of these towns I learn in what county
I have lighted; a north-midland shire, dusk with moorland, ridged with mountain: this I see. There are great
moors behind and on each hand of me; there are waves
of mountains far beyond that deep valley at my feet. The
population here must be thin, and I see no passengers
on these roads: they stretch out east, west, north, and
south—white, broad, lonely; they are all cut in the moor,
and the heather grows deep and wild to their very verge.
Yet a chance traveller might pass by; and I wish no eye
to see me now: strangers would wonder what I am doing,
lingering here at the sign-post, evidently objectless and
lost. I might be questioned: I could give no answer but
what would sound incredible and excite suspicion. Not a
tie holds me to human society at this moment—not a
charm or hope calls me where my fellow-creatures are
—none that saw me would have a kind thought or a good
wish for me. I have no relative but the universal mother,
Nature: I will seek her breast and ask repose.

I struck straight into the heath; I held on to a hollow
I saw deeply furrowing the brown moorside; I waded
knee-deep in its dark growth; I turned with its turnings,
and finding a moss-blackened granite crag in a hidden

angle, I sat down under it. High banks of moor were about me; the crag protected my head: the sky was over that.

Some time passed before I felt tranquil even here: I had a vague dread that wild cattle might be near, or that some sportsman or poacher might discover me. If a gust of wind swept the waste, I looked up, fearing it was the rush of a bull; if a plover whistled, I imagined it a man. Finding my apprehensions unfounded, however, and calmed by the deep silence that reigned as evening declined at nightfall, I took confidence. As yet I had not thought; I had only listened, watched, dreaded; now I regained the faculty of reflection.

What was I to do? Where to go? Oh, intolerable questions, when I could do nothing and go nowhere! —when a long way must yet be measured by my weary, trembling limbs before I could reach human habitation —when cold charity must be entreated before I could get a lodging: reluctant sympathy importuned, almost certain repulse incurred, before my tale could be listened to, or one of my wants relieved!

I touched the heath: it was dry, and yet warm with the heat of the summer day. I looked at the sky; it was pure: a kindly star twinkled just above the chasm ridge. The dew fell, but with propitious softness; no breeze whispered. Nature seemed to me benign and good; I thought she loved me, outcast as I was; and I, who from man could anticipate only mistrust, rejection, insult, clung to her with filial fondness. To-night, at least, I would be her guest, as I was her child: my mother would lodge me without money and without price. I had one morsel of bread yet: the remnant of a roll I had bought in a town we passed through at noon with a stray penny—my last coin. I saw ripe bilberries gleaming here and there, like jet beads in the heath: I gathered a handful and ate them with the bread. My hunger, sharp before, was, if not satisfied, appeased by this hermit's meal. I said my evening prayers at its conclusion, and then chose my couch.

Beside the crag the heath was very deep: when I lay down my feet were buried in it; rising high on each side, it left only a narrow space for the night-air to invade. I folded my shawl double, and spread it over me for a coverlet; a low, mossy swell was my pillow. Thus lodged, I was not, at least at the commencement of the night, cold.

My rest might have been blissful enough, only a sad heart broke it. It plained of its gaping wounds, its inward bleeding, its riven chords. It trembled for Mr Rochester and his doom; it bemoaned him with bitter pity; it demanded him with ceaseless longing; and, impotent as a bird with both wings broken, it still quivered its shattered pinions in vain attempts to seek him.

Worn out with this torture of thought, I rose to my knees. Night was come, and her planets were risen: a safe, still night: too serene for the companionship of fear. We know that God is everywhere; but certainly we feel His presence most when His works are on the grandest scale spread before us; and it is in the unclouded night-sky, where His worlds wheel their silent course, that we read clearest His infinitude, His omnipotence, His omnipresence. I had risen to my knees to pray for Mr Rochester. Looking up, I, with tear-dimmed eyes, saw the mighty Milky-way. Remembering what it was —what countless systems there swept space like a soft trace of light—I felt the might and strength of God. Sure was I of His efficiency to save what He had made: convinced I grew that neither earth should perish, nor one of the souls it treasured. I turned my prayer to thanksgiving: the Source of Life was also the Saviour of spirits. Mr Rochester was safe: he was God's, and by God would he be guarded. I again nestled to the breast of the hill; and ere long in sleep forgot sorrow.

But next day, Want came to me pale and bare. Long after the little birds had left their nests, long after bees had come in the sweet prime of day to gather the heath honey before the dew was dried—when the long morning shadows were curtailed, and the sun filled earth and sky —I got up, and I looked round me.

What a still, hot, perfect day! What a golden desert this spreading moor! Everywhere sunshine. I wished I could live in it and on it. I saw a lizard run over the crag; I saw a bee busy among the sweet bilberries. I would fain at the moment have become bee or lizard, that I might have found fitting nutriment, permanent shelter here. But I was a human being, and had a human being's wants: I must not linger where there was nothing to supply them. I rose; I looked back at the bed I had left. Hopeless of the future, I wished but this—that my Maker had that night thought good to require my soul of me while I slept; and that this weary frame, absolved by death from further conflict with fate, had now but to decay quietly, and mingle in peace with the soil of this wilderness. Life, however, was yet in my possession, with all its requirements, and pains, and responsibilities. The burden must be carried; the want provided for; the suffering endured; the responsibility fulfilled. I set out.

Whitcross regained, I followed a road which led from the sun, now fervent and high. By no other circumstance had I will to decide my choice. I walked a long time, and when I thought I had nearly done enough, and might conscientiously yield to the fatigue that almost over-powered me—might relax this forced action, and, sitting down on a stone I saw near, submit resistlessly to the apathy that clogged heart and limb—I heard a bell chime—a church bell.

I turned in the direction of the sound, and there, amongst the romantic hills, whose changes and aspect I had ceased to note an hour ago, I saw a hamlet and a spire. All the valley at my right hand was full of pasture-fields, and corn-fields, and wood; and a glittering stream ran zig-zag through the varied shades of green, the mellowing grain, the sombre woodland, the clear and sunny lea. Recalled by the rumbling of wheels to the road before me, I saw a heavily-laden waggon labouring up the hill, and not far beyond were two cows and their drover. Human life and human labour were near. I must struggle on: strive to live and bend to toil like the rest.

About two o'clock p.m. I entered the village. At the bottom of its one street there was a little shop with some cakes of bread in the window. I coveted a cake of bread. With that refreshment I could perhaps regain a degree of energy: without it, it would be difficult to proceed. The wish to have some strength and some vigour returned to me as soon as I was amongst my fellow-beings. I felt it would be degrading to faint with hunger on the cause-way of a hamlet. Had I nothing about me I could offer in exchange for one of these rolls? I considered. I had a small silk handkerchief tied round my throat; I had my gloves. I could hardly tell how men and women in extremities of destitution proceeded. I did not know whether either of these articles would be accepted: probably they would not; but I must try.

I entered the shop: a woman was there. Seeing a respectably-dressed person, a lady as she supposed, she came forward with civility. How could she serve me? I was seized with shame: my tongue would not utter the request I had prepared. I dared not offer her the half-worn gloves, the creased handkerchief: besides, I felt it would be absurd. I only begged permission to sit down a moment, as I was tired. Disappointed in the expecta-tion of a customer, she coolly acceded to my request. She pointed to a seat; I sank into it. I felt sorely urged to weep; but conscious how unseasonable such a mani-festation would be, I restrained it. Soon I asked her "if there were any dressmaker or plain-workwoman in the village?"

"Yes; two or three. Quite as many as there was employment for."

I reflected. I was driven to the point now. I was brought face to face with Necessity. I stood in the position of one without a resource, without a friend, without a coin. I must do something. What? I must apply somewhere. Where?

"Did she know of any place in the neighbourhood where a servant was wanted?"

"Nay; she couldn't say."

"What was the chief trade in this place? What did most of the people do?"

"Some were farm labourers; a good deal worked at Mr Oliver's needle-factory, and at the foundry."

"Did Mr Oliver employ women?"

"Nay; it was men's work."

"And what do the women do?"

"I knawn't," was the answer. "Some does one thing, and some another. Poor folk mun get on as they can."

She seemed to be tired of my questions: and, indeed, what claim had I to importune her? A neighbour or two came in; my chair was evidently wanted. I took leave.

I passed up the street, looking as I went at all the houses to the right hand and to the left; but I could discover no pretext, nor see an inducement to enter any. I rambled round the hamlet, going sometimes to a little distance and returning again, for an hour or more. Much exhausted, and suffering greatly now for want of food, I turned aside into a lane and sat down under the hedge. Ere many minutes had elapsed, I was again on my feet, however, and again searching something— a resource, or at least an informant. A pretty little house stood at the top of the lane, with a garden before it, exquisitely neat and brilliantly blooming. I stopped at it. What business had I to approach the white door or touch the glittering knocker? In what way could it possibly be the interest of the inhabitants of that dwelling to serve me? Yet I drew near and knocked. A mild-looking, cleanly-attired young woman opened the door. In such a voice as might be expected from a hopeless heart and fainting frame—a voice wretchedly low and faltering—I asked if a servant was wanted here?

"No," said she; "we do not keep a servant."

"Can you tell me where I could get employment of any kind?" I continued. "I am a stranger, without acquaintance in this place. I want some work: no matter what."

But it was not her business to think for me, or to seek a place for me: besides, in her eyes, how doubtful must have appeared my character, position, tale. She shook her head, she "was sorry she could give me no information," and the white door closed, quite gently and civilly: but it shut me out. If she had held it open a little longer, I believe I should have begged a piece of bread; for I was now brought low.

I could not bear to return to the sordid village, where, besides, no prospect of aid was visible. I should have longed rather to deviate to a wood I saw not far off, which appeared in its thick shade to offer inviting shelter; but I was so sick, so weak, so gnawed with nature's cravings, instinct kept me roaming round abodes where there was a chance of food. Solitude would be no solitude—rest no rest—while the vulture, hunger, thus sank beak and talons in my side.

I drew near houses; I left them, and came back again, and again I wandered away: always repelled by the consciousness of having no claim to ask—no right to expect interest in my isolated lot. Meantime, the afternoon advanced, while I thus wandered about like a lost and starving dog. In crossing a field, I saw the church spire before me: I hastened towards it. Near the churchyard, and in the middle of a garden, stood a well-built though small house, which I had no doubt was the parsonage. I remembered that strangers who arrive at a place where they have no friends, and who want employment, sometimes apply to the clergyman for introduction and aid. It is the clergyman's function to help—at least with advice—those who wished to help themselves. I seemed to have something like a right to seek counsel here. Renewing then my courage, and gathering my feeble remains of strength, I pushed on. I reached the house, and knocked at the kitchen-door. An old woman opened: I asked was this the parsonage?

"Yes."

"Was the clergyman in?"

"No."

"Would he be in soon?"

"No, he was gone from home."

"To a distance?"

"Not so far—happen three mile. He had been called away by the sudden death of his father: he was at Marsh End now, and would very likely stay there a fortnight longer."

"Was there any lady of the house?"

"Nay, there was naught but her, and she was house-keeper"; and of her, reader, I could not bear to ask the relief for want of which I was sinking; I could not yet beg; and again I crawled away.

Once more I took off my handkerchief—once more I thought of the cakes of bread in the little shop. Oh, for but a crust! for but one mouthful to allay the pang of famine! Instinctively I turned my face again to the village; I found the shop again, and I went in; and though others were there besides the woman I ventured the request—"Would she give me a roll for this handker-chief?"

She looked at me with evident suspicion: "Nay, she never sold stuff i' that way."

Almost desperate, I asked for half a cake; she again refused. "How could she tell where I had got the handkerchief?" she said.

"Would she take my gloves?"

"No! what could she do with them?"

Reader, it is not pleasant to dwell on these details. Some say there is enjoyment in looking back to painful experience past; but at this day I can scarcely bear to review the times to which I allude: the moral degradation, blent with the physical suffering, form too distressing a recollection ever to be willingly dwelt on. I blamed none of those who repulsed me. I felt it was what was to be expected, and what could not be helped: an ordinary beggar is frequently an object of suspicion; a well-dressed beggar inevitably so. To be sure, what I begged was employment; but whose business was it to provide me with employment? Not, certainly, that of persons who saw me then for the first time, and who knew nothing about my character. And as to the woman who would not take my handkerchief in exchange for her bread, why, she was right, if the offer appeared to her sinister or the exchange unprofitable. Let me condense now. I am sick of the subject.

A little before dark I passed a farmhouse, at the open door of which the farmer was sitting, eating his supper of bread and cheese. I stopped and said—

"Will you give me a piece of bread? for I am very hungry." He cast on me a glance of surprise; but without answering, he cut a thick slice from his loaf, and gave it to me. I imagine he did not think I was a beggar, but only an eccentric sort of lady, who had taken a fancy to his brown loaf. As soon as I was out of sight of his house, I sat down and ate it.

I could not hope to get a lodging under a roof, and sought it in the wood I have before alluded to. But my night was wretched, my rest broken: the ground was damp, the air cold: besides, intruders passed near me more than once, and I had again and again to change my quarters: no sense of safety or tranquillity befriended me. Towards morning it rained; the whole of the following day was wet. Do not ask me, reader, to give a minute account of that day; as before, I sought work; as before, I was repulsed; as before, I starved; but once did food pass my lips. At the door of a cottage I saw a little girl about to throw a mess of cold porridge into a pig trough. "Will you give me that?" I asked.

She stared at me. "Mother!" she exclaimed, "there is a woman wants me to give her these porridge."

"Well, lass," replied a voice within, "give it her if she's a beggar. T' pig doesn't want it."

The girl emptied the stiffened mould into my hand, and I devoured it ravenously.

As the wet twilight deepened, I stopped in a solitary bridle-path, which I had been pursuing an hour or more.

"My strength is quite failing me," I said in a soliloquy. "I feel I cannot go much farther. Shall I be an outcast again this night? While the rain descends so, must I lay my head on the cold, drenched ground? I fear I cannot do otherwise: for who will receive me? But it will be very dreadful, with this feeling of hunger, faintness, chill, and this sense of desolation—this total prostration of hope. In all likelihood, though, I should die before morning. And why cannot I reconcile myself to the prospect of death? Why do I struggle to retain a valueless life? Because I know, or believe, Mr Rochester is living: and then, to die of want and cold is a fate to which nature cannot submit passively. Oh, Providence! sustain me a little longer! Aid!—direct me!"

My glazed eye wandered over the dim and misty landscape. I saw I had strayed far from the village: it was quite out of sight. The very cultivation surrounding it had disappeared. I had, by cross-ways and by-paths, once more drawn near the tract of moorland; and now, only a few fields, almost as wild and unproductive as the heath from which they were scarcely reclaimed, lay between me and the dusky hill.

"Well, I would rather die yonder than in a street or on a frequented road," I reflected. "And far better that crows and ravens—if any ravens there be in these regions —should pick my flesh from my bones, than that they should be prisoned in a workhouse coffin and moulder in a pauper's grave."

To the hill, then, I turned. I reached it. It remained now only to find a hollow where I could lie down, and feel at least hidden, if not secure. But all the surface of the waste looked level. It showed no variation but of tint: green, where rush and moss overgrew the marshes; black, where the dry soil bore only heath. Dark as it was getting, I could still see these changes, though but as mere alternations of light and shade; for colour had faded with the daylight.

My eye still roved over the sullen swell and along the moor-edge, vanishing amidst the wildest scenery, when at one dim point, far in among the marshes and the ridges, a light sprang up. "That is an *ignis fatuus*," was my first thought; and I expected it would soon vanish. It burnt on, however, quite steadily, neither receding nor advancing. "Is it, then, a bonfire just kindled?" I questioned. I watched to see whether it would spread: but no; as it did not diminish, so it did not enlarge. "It may be a candle in a house," I then conjectured; "but if so, I can never reach it. It is much too far away: and were it within a yard of me, what would it avail? I should but knock at the door to have it shut in my face."

And I sank down where I stood, and hid my face against the ground. I lay still a while: the night-wind swept over the hill and over me, and died moaning in the distance; the rain fell fast, wetting me afresh to the skin. Could I but have stiffened to the still frost—the friendly numbness of death—it might have pelted on;

I should not have felt it; but my yet living flesh shuddered at its chilling influence. I rose ere long.

The light was yet there, shining dim but constant through the rain. I tried to walk again: I dragged my exhausted limbs slowly towards it. It led me aslant over the hill, through a wide bog, which would have been impassable in winter, and was splashy and shaking even now, in the height of summer. Here I fell twice; but as often I rose and rallied my faculties. This light was my forlorn hope: I must gain it.

Having crossed the marsh, I saw a trace of white over the moor. I approached it; it was a road or a track: it led straight up to the light, which now beamed from a sort of knoll, amidst a clump of trees—firs, apparently, from what I could distinguish of the character of their forms and foliage through the gloom. My star vanished as I drew near: some obstacle had intervened between me and it. I put out my hand to feel the dark mass before me: I discriminated the rough stones of a low wall —above it, something like palisades, and within, a high and prickly hedge. I groped on. Again a whitish object gleamed before me: it was a gate—a wicket; it moved on its hinges as I touched it. On each side stood a sable bush—holly or yew.

Entering the gate and passing the shrubs, the silhouette of a house rose to view, black, low, and rather long; but the guiding light shone nowhere. All was obscurity. Were the inmates retired to rest? I feared it must be so. In seeking the door, I turned an angle: there shot out the friendly gleam again, from the lozenged panes of a very small latticed window, within a foot of the ground, made still smaller by the growth of ivy or some other creeping plant, whose leaves clustered thick over the portion of the house wall in which it was set. The aperture was so screened and narrow, that curtain or shutter had been deemed unnecessary; and when I stooped down and put aside the spray of foliage shooting over it, I could see all within. I could see clearly a room with a sanded floor, clean scoured; a dresser of walnut, with pewter plates ranged in rows, reflecting the redness and radiance of a glowing peat-fire. I could see a clock, a white deal table, some chairs. The candle, whose ray had been my beacon, burnt on the table; and by its light an elderly woman, somewhat rough-looking, but scrupulously clean, like all about her, was knitting a stocking.

I noticed these objects cursorily only—in them there was nothing extraordinary. A group of more interest appeared near the hearth, sitting still amidst the rosy peace and warmth suffusing it. Two young, graceful women—ladies in every point—sat, one in a low rocking-chair, the other on a lower stool; both wore deep mourning of crape and bombazeen, which sombre garb singularly set off very fair necks and faces: a large old pointer dog rested its massive head on the knee of one girl—in the lap of the other was cushioned a black cat.

A strange place was this humble kitchen for such occupants! Who were they? They could not be the daughters of the elderly person at the table; for she looked like a rustic, and they were all delicacy and cultivation. I had nowhere seen such faces as theirs: and yet, as I gazed on them, I seemed intimate with every lineament. I cannot call them handsome—they were too pale and grave for the word: as they each bent over a book, they looked thoughtful almost to severity. A stand between them supported a second candle and two great volumes, to which they frequently referred, comparing them, seemingly, with the smaller books they held in their hands, like people consulting a dictionary to aid them in the task of translation. This scene was as silent as if all the figures had been shadows and the firelit apartment a picture: so hushed was it, I could hear the cinders fall from the grate, the clock tick in its obscure corner; and I even fancied I could distinguish the click-click of the woman's knitting-needles. When, therefore, a voice

broke the strange stillness at last, it was audible enough
to me.

"Listen, Diana," said one of the absorbed students;
"Franz and old Daniel are together in the night-time,
and Franz is telling a dream from which he has awakened
in terror—listen!" And in a low voice she read something, of which not one word was intelligible to me;
for it was in an unknown tongue—neither French nor
Latin. Whether it were Greek or German I could not
tell.

"That is strong," she said, when she had finished:
"I relish it." The other girl, who had lifted her head to
listen to her sister, repeated, while she gazed at the fire,
a line of what had been read. At a later day, I knew the
language and the book; therefore, I will here quote the
line: though, when I first heard it, it was only like a stroke
on sounding brass to me—conveying no meaning:

"'Da trat hervor Einer, anzusehen wie die Sternen
Nacht.' Good! good!" she exclaimed, while her dark
and deep eye sparkled. "There you have a dim and
mighty archangel fitly set before you! The line is worth
a hundred pages of fustian. 'Ich wäge die Gedanken in
der Schale meines Zornes und die Werke mit dem
Gewichte meines Grimms.' I like it!"

Both were again silent.

"Is there any country where they talk i' that way?"
asked the old woman, looking up from her knitting.

"Yes, Hannah—a far larger country than England,
where they talk in no other way."

"Well, for sure case, I knawn't how they can understand t'one t'other: and if either o' ye went there, ye
could tell what they said, I guess?"

"We could probably tell something of what they said,
but not all—for we are not as clever as you think us,
Hannah. We don't speak German, and we cannot read
it without a dictionary to help us."

"And what good does it do you?"

"We mean to teach it some time—or at least the elements, as they say; and then we shall get more money than we do now."

"Varry like: but give ower studying; ye've done enough for to-night."

"I think we have: at least I'm tired. Mary, are you?"

"Mortally: after all, it's tough work fagging away at a language with no master but a lexicon."

"It is, especially such a language as this crabbed but glorious Deutsch. I wonder when St John will come home."

"Surely he will not be long now: it is just ten (looking at a little gold watch she drew from her girdle). It rains fast, Hannah: will you have the goodness to look at the fire in the parlour?"

The woman rose: she opened a door, through which I dimly saw a passage: soon I heard her stir a fire in an inner room; she presently came back.

"Ah, childer!" said she, "it fair troubles me to go into yond' room now: it looks so lonesome wi' the chair empty and set back in a corner."

She wiped her eyes with her apron: the two girls, grave before, looked sad now.

"But he is in a better place," continued Hannah: "we shouldn't wish him here again. And then, nobody need to have a quieter death nor he had."

"You say he never mentioned us?" inquired one of the ladies.

"He hadn't time, bairn: he was gone in a minute, was your father. He had been a bit ailing like the day before, but naught to signify; and when Mr St John asked if he would like either o' ye to be sent for, he fair laughed at him. He began again with a bit of a heaviness in his head the next day—that is, a fortnight sin'—and he went to sleep and niver wakened: he wor a'most stark when your brother went into t' chamber and fand him. Ah, childer! that's t' last o' t' old stock—for ye and Mr St John is like

of different soart to them 'at's gone; for all your mother
wor mich i' your way, and a'most as book-learned. She
wor the pictur' o' ye, Mary: Diana is more like your
father."

I thought them so similar I could not tell where the
old servant (for such I now concluded her to be) saw the
difference. Both were fair complexioned and slenderly
made; both possessed faces full of distinction and intelligence. One, to be sure, had hair a shade darker than
the other, and there was a difference in their style of
wearing it; Mary's pale brown locks were parted and
braided smooth: Diana's duskier tresses covered her neck
with thick curls. The clock struck ten.

"Ye'll want your supper, I am sure," observed
Hannah; "and so will Mr St John when he comes
in."

And she proceeded to prepare the meal. The ladies
rose; they seemed about to withdraw to the parlour. Till
this moment, I had been so intent on watching them,
their appearance and conversation had excited in me so
keen an interest, I had half-forgotten my own wretched
position: now it recurred to me. More desolate, more
desperate than ever, it seemed from contrast. And how
impossible did it appear to touch the inmates of this
house with concern on my behalf; to make them believe
in the truth of my wants and woes—to induce them to
vouchsafe a rest for my wanderings! As I groped out
the door, and knocked at it hesitatingly, I felt that last
idea to be a mere chimera. Hannah opened.

"What do you want?" she inquired, in a voice of
surprise, as she surveyed me by the light of the candle
she held.

"May I speak to your mistresses?" I said.

"You had better tell me what you have to say to them.
Where do you come from?"

"I am a stranger."

"What is your business here at this hour?"

"I want a night's shelter in an out-house or anywhere, and a morsel of bread to eat."

Distrust, the very feeling I dreaded, appeared in Hannah's face. "I'll give you a piece of bread," she said, after a pause; "but we can't take in a vagrant to lodge. It isn't likely."

"Do let me speak to your mistresses."

"No, not I. What can they do for you? You should not be roving about now; it looks very ill."

"But where shall I go if you drive me away? What shall I do?"

"Oh, I'll warrant you know where to go and what to do. Mind you don't do wrong, that's all. Here is a penny; now go——"

"A penny cannot feed me, and I have no strength to go farther. Don't shut the door:—oh, don't, for God's sake!"

"I must; the rain is driving in——"

"Tell the young ladies. Let me see them——"

"Indeed, I will not. You are not what you ought to be, or you wouldn't make such a noise. Move off."

"But I must die if I am turned away."

"Not you. I'm fear'd you have some ill plans agate, that bring you about folk's houses at this time o' night. If you've any followers—housebreakers or such like—anywhere near, you may tell them we are not by ourselves in the house; we have a gentleman, and dogs, and guns." Here the honest but inflexible servant clapped the door to and bolted it within.

This was the climax. A pang of exquisite suffering—a throe of true despair—rent and heaved my heart. Worn out, indeed, I was; not another step could I stir. I sank on the wet doorstep: I groaned—I wrung my hands—I wept in utter anguish. Oh, this spectre of death! Oh, this last hour, approaching in such horror! Alas, this isolation—this banishment from my kind! Not only the anchor of hope, but the footing of fortitude was gone—

at least for a moment; but the last I soon endeavoured to regain.

"I can but die," I said, "and I believe in God. Let me try to wait His will in silence."

These words I not only thought, but uttered; and thrusting back all my misery into my heart, I made an effort to compel it to remain there—dumb and still.

"All men must die," said a voice quite close at hand; "but all are not condemned to meet a lingering and premature doom, such as yours would be if you perished here of want."

"Who or what speaks?" I asked, terrified at the unexpected sound, and incapable now of deriving from any occurrence a hope of aid. A form was near—what form, the pitch-dark night and my enfeebled vision prevented me from distinguishing. With a loud long knock, the new-comer appealed to the door.

"Is it you, Mr St John?" cried Hannah.

"Yes—yes; open quickly."

"Well, how wet and cold you must be, such a wild night as it is! Come in—your sisters are quite uneasy about you, and I believe there are bad folks about. There has been a beggar-woman—I declare she is not gone yet! —laid down there. Get up! for shame! Move off, I say!"

"Hush, Hannah! I have a word to say to the woman. You have done your duty in excluding, now let me do mine in admitting her. I was near, and listened to both you and her. I think this is a peculiar case—I must at least examine into it. Young woman, rise, and pass before me into the house."

With difficulty I obeyed him. Presently I stood within that clean, bright kitchen—on the very hearth—trembling, sickening; conscious of an aspect in the last degree ghastly, wild, and weather-beaten. The two ladies, their brother, Mr St John, the old servant, were all gazing at me.

"St John, who is it?" I heard one ask.

"I cannot tell: I found her at the door," was the reply.

"She does look white," said Hannah.

"As white as clay or death," was responded. "She will fall: let her sit."

And indeed my head swam: I dropped, but a chair received me. I still possessed my senses, though just now I could not speak.

"Perhaps a little water would restore her. Hannah, fetch some. But she is worn to nothing. How very thin, and how very bloodless!"

"A mere spectre!"

"Is she ill, or only famished?"

"Famished, I think. Hannah, is that milk? Give it me, and a piece of bread."

Diana (I knew her by the long curls which I saw drooping between me and the fire as she bent over me) broke some bread, dipped it in milk, and put it to my lips. Her face was near mine: I saw there was pity in it, and I felt sympathy in her hurried breathing. In her simple words, too, the same balm-like emotion spoke: "Try to eat."

"Yes—try," repeated Mary gently; and Mary's hand removed my sodden bonnet and lifted my head. I tasted what they offered me: feebly at first, eagerly soon.

"Not too much at first—restrain her," said the brother; "she has had enough." And he withdrew the cup of milk and the plate of bread.

"A little more, St John—look at the avidity in her eyes."

"No more at present, sister. Try if she can speak now —ask her her name."

I felt I could speak, and I answered—"My name is Jane Elliott." Anxious as ever to avoid discovery, I had before resolved to assume an *alias*.

"And where do you live? Where are your friends?"

I was silent.

"Can we send for any one you know?"

T   7

I shook my head.

"What account can you give of yourself?"

Somehow, now that I had once crossed the threshold of this house, and once was brought face to face with its owners, I felt no longer outcast, vagrant, and disowned by the wide world. I dared to put off the mendicant—to resume my natural manner and character. I began once more to know myself; and when Mr St John demanded an account—which at present I was far too weak to render—I said after a brief pause—

"Sir, I can give you no details to-night."

"But what, then," said he, "do you expect me to do for you?"

"Nothing," I replied. My strength sufficed for but short answers. Diana took the word—

"Do you mean," she asked, "that we have now given you what aid you require? and that we may dismiss you to the moor and the rainy night?"

I looked at her. She had, I thought, a remarkable countenance, instinct both with power and goodness. I took sudden courage. Answering her compassionate gaze with a smile, I said—"I will trust you. If I were a masterless and stray dog, I know that you would not turn me from your hearth to-night: as it is, I really have no fear. Do with me and for me as you like; but excuse me from much discourse—my breath is short—I feel a spasm when I speak." All three surveyed me, and all three were silent.

"Hannah," said Mr St John, at last, "let her sit there at present, and ask her no questions; in ten minutes more, give her the remainder of that milk and bread. Mary and Diana, let us go into the parlour and talk the matter over."

They withdrew. Very soon one of the ladies returned —I could not tell which. A kind of pleasant stupor was stealing over me as I sat by the genial fire. In an undertone she gave some directions to Hannah. Ere long,

with the servant's aid, I contrived to mount a staircase;
my dripping clothes were removed; soon a warm, dry
bed received me. I thanked God—experienced amidst
unutterable exhaustion a glow of grateful joy—and slept.

HOME AT LAST

from *Jane Eyre*.

I LEFT Moor House at three o'clock p.m., and soon
after four I stood at the foot of the sign-post of Whitcross, waiting the arrival of the coach which was to take
me to distant Thornfield. Amidst the silence of those
solitary roads and desert hills, I heard it approach from
a great distance. It was the same vehicle whence, a year
ago, I had alighted one summer evening on this very
spot—how desolate, and hopeless, and objectless! It
stopped as I beckoned. I entered—not now obliged to
part with my whole fortune as the price of its accommodation. Once more on the road to Thornfield, I felt like
the messenger-pigeon flying home.

It was a journey of six-and-thirty hours. I had set out
from Whitcross on a Tuesday afternoon, and early on
the succeeding Thursday morning the coach stopped to
water the horses at a wayside inn, situated in the midst
of scenery whose green hedges and large fields and low
pastoral hills (how mild of feature and verdant of hue
compared with the stern North-Midland moors of
Morton!) met my eye like the lineaments of a once
familiar face. Yes, I knew the character of this landscape:
I was sure we were near my bourne.

"How far is Thornfield Hall from here?" I asked of the
ostler.

"Just two miles, ma'am, across the fields."

"My journey is closed," I thought to myself. I got out
of the coach, gave a box I had into the ostler's charge,
to be kept till I called for it; paid my fare; satisfied the

coachman, and was going: the brightening day gleamed
on the sign of the inn, and I read in gilt letters, "The
Rochester Arms." My heart leapt up: I was already on
my master's very lands. It fell again: the thought
struck it:

"Your master himself may be beyond the British
Channel, for aught you know: and then, if he is at
Thornfield Hall, towards which you hasten, who besides
him is there? His lunatic wife: and you have nothing
to do with him: you dare not speak to him or seek his
presence. You have lost your labour—you had better
go no farther," urged the monitor. "Ask information
of the people at the inn; they can give you all you seek:
they can solve your doubts at once. Go up to that man,
and inquire if Mr Rochester be at home."

The suggestion was sensible, and yet I could not force
myself to act on it. I so dreaded a reply that would crush
me with despair. To prolong doubt was to prolong hope.
I might yet once more see the Hall under the ray of her
star. There was the stile before me—the very fields through
which I had hurried, blind, deaf, distracted with a re-
vengeful fury tracking and scourging me, on the morning
I fled from Thornfield: ere I well knew what course I had
resolved to take, I was in the midst of them. How fast
I walked! How I ran sometimes! How I looked forward
to catch the first view of the well-known woods! With
what feelings I welcomed single trees I knew, and familiar
glimpses of meadow and hill between them!

At last the woods rose; the rookery clustered dark;
a loud cawing broke the morning stillness. Strange
delight inspired me: on I hastened. Another field crossed
—a lane threaded—and there were the courtyard walls
—the back offices: the house itself, the rookery still hid.
"My first view of it shall be in front," I determined,
"where its bold battlements will strike the eye nobly at
once, and where I can single out my master's very
window: perhaps he will be standing at it—he rises early:

perhaps he is now walking in the orchard, or on the pavement in front. Could I but see him!—but a moment! Surely, in that case, I should not be so mad as to run to him? I cannot tell—I am not certain. And if I did—what then? God bless him! What then? Who would be hurt by my once more tasting the life his glance can give me? I rave: perhaps at this moment he is watching the sun rise over the Pyrenees, or on the tideless sea of the south."

I had coasted along the lower wall of the orchard—turned its angle: there was a gate just there, opening into the meadow, between two stone pillars crowned by stone balls. From behind one pillar I could peep round quietly at the full front of the mansion. I advanced my head with precaution, desirous to ascertain if any bedroom window-blinds were yet drawn up: battlements, windows, long front—all from this sheltered station were at my command.

The crows sailing overhead perhaps watched me while I took this survey. I wonder what they thought. They must have considered I was very careful and timid at first, and that gradually I grew very bold and reckless. A peep, and then a long stare; and then a departure from my niche and a straying out into the meadow; and a sudden stop full in front of the great mansion, and a protracted, hardy gaze towards it. "What affectation of diffidence was this at first?" they might have demanded; "what stupid regardlessness now?"

Hear an illustration, reader.

A lover finds his mistress asleep on a mossy bank; he wishes to catch a glimpse of her fair face without waking her. He steals softly over the grass, careful to make no sound; he pauses—fancying she has stirred: he withdraws: not for worlds would he be seen. All is still: he again advances: he bends above her; a light veil rests on her features: he lifts it, bends lower; now his eyes anticipate the vision of beauty—warm, and blooming, and lovely, in rest. How hurried was their first glance! But how they fix! How he starts! How he suddenly and vehemently clasps in both arms the form he dared not, a moment since, touch with his finger! How he calls aloud a name, and drops his burden, and gazes on it wildly! He thus grasps and cries, and gazes, because he no longer fears to waken by any sound he can utter—by any movement he can make. He thought his love slept sweetly: he finds she is stone dead.

I looked with timorous joy towards a stately house: I saw a blackened ruin.

No need to cower behind a gate-post, indeed!—to peep up at chamber lattices, fearing life was astir behind them! No need to listen for doors opening—to fancy steps on the pavement or the gravel-walk! The lawn, the grounds were trodden and waste: the portal yawned void. The front was, as I had once seen it in a dream, but a shell-like wall, very high and very fragile-looking, perforated with paneless windows: no roof, no battlements, no chimneys—all had crashed in.

And there was the silence of death about it: the solitude of a lonesome wild. No wonder that letters addressed to people here had never received an answer: as well despatch epistles to a vault in a church aisle. The grim blackness of the stones told by what fate the Hall had fallen—by conflagration: but how kindled? What story belonged to this disaster? What loss, besides mortar and marble and woodwork, had followed upon it? Had life been wrecked as well as property? If so, whose? Dreadful question: there was no one here to answer it—not even dumb sign, mute token.

In wandering round the shattered walls and through the devastated interior, I gathered evidence that the calamity was not of late occurrence. Winter snows, I thought, had drifted through that void arch, winter rains beaten in at those hollow casements; for, amidst the drenched piles of rubbish, spring had cherished vegetation: grass and weed grew here and there between the stones and fallen rafters. And oh! where meantime was the hapless owner of this wreck? In what land? Under what auspices? My eye involuntarily wandered to the grey church tower near the gates, and I asked, "Is he with Damer de Rochester, sharing the shelter of his narrow marble house?"

Some answer must be had to these questions. I could find it nowhere but at the inn, and thither, ere long, I returned. The host himself brought my breakfast into the parlour. I requested him to shut the door and sit down: I had some questions to ask him. But when he complied, I scarcely knew how to begin; such horror had I of the possible answers. And yet the spectacle of desolation I had just left prepared me in a measure for a tale of misery. The host was a respectable-looking, middle-aged man.

"You know Thornfield Hall, of course?" I managed to say at last.

"Yes, ma'am; I lived there once."

"Did you?" Not in my time, I thought: you are a stranger to me.

"I was the late Mr Rochester's butler," he added.

The late! I seem to have received, with full force, the blow I had been trying to evade.

"The late!" I gasped. "Is he dead?"

"I mean the present gentleman, Mr Edward's father," he explained. I breathed again: my blood resumed its flow. Fully assured by these words that Mr Edward— *my* Mr Rochester (God bless him, wherever he was!)— was at least alive: was, in short, "the present gentleman." Gladdening words! It seemed I could hear all that was to come—whatever the disclosures might be—with comparative tranquillity. Since he was not in the grave, I could bear, I thought, to learn that he was at the Antipodes.

"Is Mr Rochester living at Thornfield Hall now?"

I asked, knowing, of course, what the answer would be, but yet desirous of deferring the direct question as to where he really was.

"No, ma'am—oh, no! No one is living there. I suppose you are a stranger in these parts, or you would have heard what happened last autumn,—Thornfield Hall is quite a ruin: it was burnt down just about harvest-time. A dreadful calamity! such an immense quantity of valuable property destroyed: hardly any of the furniture could be saved. The fire broke out at dead of night, and before the engines arrived from Millcote, the building was one mass of flame. It was a terrible spectacle: I witnessed it myself."

"At dead of night!" I muttered. Yes, that was ever the hour of fatality at Thornfield. "Was it known how it originated?" I demanded.

"They guessed, ma'am: they guessed. Indeed, I should say it was ascertained beyond a doubt. You are not perhaps aware," he continued, edging his chair a little nearer the table, and speaking low, "that there was a lady—a—a lunatic, kept in the house?... This lady, ma'am, turned out to be Mr Rochester's wife! The discovery was brought about in the strangest way. There was a young lady, a governess at the Hall, that Mr Rochester fell in——"

"But the fire," I suggested.

"I'm coming to that, ma'am—that Mr Edward fell in love with. The servants say they never saw anybody so much in love as he was: he was after her continually. They used to watch him—servants will, you know, ma'am —and he set store on her past everything: for all, nobody but him thought her so very handsome. She was a little small thing, they say, almost like a child. I never saw her myself; but I've heard Leah, the housemaid, tell of her. Leah liked her well enough. Mr Rochester was about forty, and this governess not twenty; and you see, when gentlemen of his age fall in love with girls, they

are often like as if they were bewitched. Well, he would
marry her."

"You shall tell me this part of the story another time,"
I said; "but now I have a particular reason for wishing
to hear all about the fire. Was it suspected that this
lunatic, Mrs Rochester, had any hand in it?"

"You've hit it, ma'am: it's quite certain that it was
her, and nobody but her, that set it going. She had
a woman to take care of her called Mrs Poole—an able
woman in her line, and very trustworthy, but for one
fault—a fault common to a deal of them nurses and
matrons—*she kept a private bottle of gin by her*, and now and
then took a drop over-much. It is excusable, for she had
a hard life of it: but still it was dangerous; for when
Mrs Poole was fast asleep after the gin and water, the
mad lady, who was as cunning as a witch, would take
the keys out of her pocket, let herself out of her chamber,
and go roaming about the house, doing any wild mischief
that came into her head. They say she had nearly burnt
her husband in his bed once: but I don't know about that.
However, on this night, she set fire first to the hangings
of the room next her own, and then she got down to
a lower storey, and made her way to the chamber that
had been the governess's—(she was like as if she knew
somehow how matters had gone on, and had a spite at
her)—and she kindled the bed there; but there was
nobody sleeping in it, fortunately. The governess had
run away two months before; and for all Mr Rochester
sought her as if she had been the most precious thing he
had in the world, he never could hear a word of her; and
he grew savage—quite savage on his disappointment:
he never was a wild man, but he got dangerous after
he lost her. He would be alone, too. He sent Mrs Fairfax,
the house-keeper, away to her friends at a distance; but
he did it handsomely, for he settled an annuity on her for
life: and she deserved it—she was a very good woman.
Miss Adèle, a ward he had, was put to school. He broke

off acquaintance with all the gentry, and shut himself
up like a hermit at the Hall."

"What! did he not leave England?"

"Leave England? Bless you, no! He would not cross
the door-stones of the house, except at night, when he
walked just like a ghost about the grounds and in the
orchard as if he had lost his senses—which it is my opinion
he had; for a more spirited, bolder, keener gentleman
than he was before that midge of a governess crossed him,
you never saw, ma'am. He was not a man given to wine,
or cards, or racing, as some are, and he was not so very
handsome; but he had a courage and a will of his own,
if ever man had. I knew him from a boy, you see: and
for my part, I have often wished that Miss Eyre had been
sunk in the sea before she came to Thornfield Hall."

"Then Mr Rochester was at home when the fire broke
out?"

"Yes, indeed was he; and he went up to the attics
when all was burning above and below, and got the
servants out of their beds and helped them down himself,
and went back to get his mad wife out of her cell. And
then they called out to him that she was on the roof,
where she was standing, waving her arms, above the
battlements, and shouting out till they could hear her
a mile off: I saw her and heard her with my own eyes.
She was a big woman, and had long black hair: we could
see it streaming against the flames as she stood. I witnessed,
and several more witnessed, Mr Rochester ascend
through the skylight on to the roof; we heard him call
'Bertha!' We saw him approach her; and then, ma'am,
she yelled and gave a spring, and the next minute she lay
smashed on the pavement."

"Dead?"

"Dead! Ay, dead as the stones on which her brains
and blood were scattered."

"Good God!"

"You may well say so, ma'am: it was frightful!"

He shuddered.

"And afterwards?" I urged.

"Well, ma'am, afterwards the house was burnt to the ground: there are only some bits of walls standing now."

"Were any other lives lost?"

"No—perhaps it would have been better if there had."

"What do you mean?"

"Poor Mr Edward!" he ejaculated, "I little thought ever to have seen it! Some say it was a just judgment on him for keeping his first marriage a secret, and wanting to take another wife while he had one living: but I pity him, for my part."

"You said he was alive?" I exclaimed.

"Yes, yes: he is alive; but many think he had better be dead."

"Why? How?" My blood was again running cold. "Where is he?" I demanded. "Is he in England?"

"Ay—ay—he's in England; he can't get out of England, I fancy—he's a fixture now."

What agony was this! And the man seemed resolved to protract it.

"He is stone-blind," he said at last. "Yes, he is stone-blind, is Mr Edward."

I had dreaded worse. I had dreaded he was mad. I summoned strength to ask what had caused this calamity.

"It was all his own courage, and a body may say, his kindness, in a way, ma'am: he wouldn't leave the house till every one else was out before him. As he came down the great staircase at last, after Mrs Rochester had flung herself from the battlements, there was a great crash—all fell. He was taken out from under the ruins, alive, but sadly hurt: a beam had fallen in such a way as to protect him partly; but one eye was knocked out, and one hand so crushed that Mr Carter, the surgeon, had to amputate it directly. The other eye inflamed: he lost the sight of that also. He is now helpless, indeed—blind and a cripple."

"Where is he? Where does he now live?"

"At Ferndean, a manor-house on a farm he has, about thirty miles off: quite a desolate spot."

"Who is with him?"

"Old John and his wife: he would have none else. He is quite broken down, they say."

"Have you any sort of conveyance?"

"We have a chaise, ma'am, a very handsome chaise."

"Let it be got ready instantly; and if your post-boy can drive me to Ferndean before dark this day, I'll pay both you and him twice the hire you usually demand."

The manor-house of Ferndean was a building of considerable antiquity, moderate size, and no architectural pretensions, deep buried in a wood. I had heard of it before. Mr Rochester often spoke of it, and sometimes went there. His father had purchased the estate for the sake of the game covers. He would have let the house, but could find no tenant, in consequence of its ineligible and insalubrious site. Ferndean then remained uninhabited and unfurnished, with the exception of some two or three rooms fitted up for the accommodation of the squire when he went there in the season to shoot.

To this house I came just ere dark on an evening marked by the characteristics of sad sky, cold gale, and continued small penetrating rain. The last mile I performed on foot, having dismissed the chaise and driver with the double remuneration I had promised. Even when within a very short distance of the manor-house, you could see nothing of it, so thick and dark grew the timber of the gloomy wood about it. Iron gates between granite pillars showed me where to enter, and passing through them, I found myself at once in the twilight of close-ranked trees. There was a grass-grown track descending the forest aisle between hoar and knotty shafts and under branched arches. I followed it, expecting soon to reach the dwelling; but it stretched on and on, it wound far and farther: no sign of habitation or grounds was visible.

I thought I had taken a wrong direction and lost my way. The darkness of natural as well as of sylvan dusk gathered over me. I looked round in search of another road. There was none: all was interwoven stem, columnar trunk, dense summer foliage—no opening anywhere.

I proceeded: at last my way opened, the trees thinned a little; presently I beheld a railing, then the house—scarce, by this dim light, distinguishable from the trees, so dank and green were its decaying walls. Entering a portal, fastened only by a latch, I stood amidst a space of enclosed ground, from which the wood swept away in a semicircle. There were no flowers, no garden-beds; only a broad gravel-walk girdling a grass-plat, and this set in the heavy frame of the forest. The house presented two pointed gables in its front; the windows were latticed and narrow: the front door was narrow too, one step led up to it. The whole looked, as the host of the Rochester Arms had said, "quite a desolate spot." It was as still as a church on a week-day: the pattering rain on the forest leaves was the only sound audible in its vicinage.

"Can there be life here?" I asked.

Yes, life of some kind there was; for I heard a movement—that narrow front-door was unclosing, and some shape was about to issue from the grange.

It opened slowly: a figure came out into the twilight and stood on the step; a man without a hat: he stretched forth his hand as if to feel whether it rained. Dusk as it was, I had recognised him—it was my master, Edward Fairfax Rochester, and no other.

I stayed my step, almost my breath, and stood to watch him—to examine him, myself unseen, and alas! to him invisible. It was a sudden meeting, and one in which rapture was kept well in check by pain. I had no difficulty in restraining my voice from exclamation, my step from hasty advance.

His form was of the same strong and stalwart contour as ever: his port was still erect, his hair was still raven black; nor were his features altered or sunk: not in one year's space, by any sorrow, could his athletic strength be quelled or his vigorous prime blighted. But in his countenance I saw a change: that looked desperate and brooding—that reminded me of some wronged and fettered wild beast or bird, dangerous to approach in his sullen woe. The caged eagle, whose gold-ringed eyes cruelty has extinguished, might look as looked that sightless Samson.

And, reader, do you think I feared him in his blind ferocity?—if you do, you little know me. A soft hope blent with my sorrow that soon I should dare to drop a kiss on that brow of rock, and on those lips so sternly sealed beneath it: but not yet. I would not accost him yet.

He descended the one step, and advanced slowly and gropingly towards the grass-plat. Where was his daring stride now? Then he paused, as if he knew not which way to turn. He lifted his hand and opened his eyelids; gazed blank, and with a straining effort, on the sky, and toward the amphitheatre of trees: one saw that all to him was void darkness. He stretched his right hand (the left arm, the mutilated one, he kept hidden in his bosom); he seemed to wish by touch to gain an idea of what lay around him: he met but vacancy still; for the trees were some yards off where he stood. He relinquished the endeavour, folded his arms, and stood quiet and mute in the rain, now falling fast on his uncovered head. At this moment John approached him from some quarter.

"Will you take my arm, sir?" he said; "there is a heavy shower coming on: had you not better go in?"

"Let me alone," was the answer.

John withdrew without having observed me. Mr Rochester now tried to walk about; vainly,—all was too uncertain. He groped his way back to the house, and, re-entering it, closed the door.

I now drew near and knocked: John's wife opened for me. "Mary," I said, "how are you?"

She started as if she had seen a ghost: I calmed her. To her hurried "Is it really you, miss, come at this late hour to this lonely place?" I answered by taking her hand; and then I followed her into the kitchen, where John now sat by a good fire. I explained to them, in few words, that I had heard all which had happened since I left Thornfield, and that I was come to see Mr Rochester. I asked John to go down to the turnpike-house, where I had dismissed the chaise, and bring my trunk, which I had left there: and then, while I removed my bonnet and shawl, I questioned Mary as to whether I could be accommodated at the Manor House for the night; and finding that arrangements to that effect, though difficult, would not be impossible, I informed her I should stay. Just at this moment the parlour-bell rang.

"When you go in," said I, "tell your master that a person wishes to speak to him, but do not give my name."

"I don't think he will see you," she answered; "he refuses everybody."

When she returned, I inquired what he had said.

"You are to send in your name and your business," she replied. She then proceeded to fill a glass with water, and place it on a tray, together with candles.

"Is that what he rang for?" I asked.

"Yes: he always has candles brought in at dark, though he is blind."

"Give the tray to me; I will carry it in."

I took it from her hand: she pointed me out the parlour door. The tray shook as I held it; the water spilt from the glass; my heart struck my ribs loud and fast. Mary opened the door for me, and shut it behind me.

This parlour looked gloomy: a neglected handful of fire burnt low in the grate; and, leaning over it, with his head supported against the high, old-fashioned mantelpiece, appeared the blind tenant of the room. His old dog, Pilot, lay on one side, removed out of the way, and coiled up as if afraid of being inadvertently trodden upon. Pilot pricked up his ears when I came in: then he jumped up with a yelp and a whine, and bounded towards me: he almost knocked the tray from my hands. I set it on the table; then patted him, and said softly, "Lie down!" Mr Rochester turned mechanically to *see* what the commotion was: but as he *saw* nothing, he returned and sighed.

"Give me the water, Mary," he said.

I approached him with the now only half-filled glass; Pilot followed me, still excited.

"What is the matter?" he inquired.

"Down, Pilot!" I again said. He checked the water on its way to his lips, and seemed to listen: he drank, and put the glass down. "This is you, Mary, is it not?"

"Mary is in the kitchen," I answered.

He put out his hand with a quick gesture, but not seeing where I stood, he did not touch me. "Who is this? Who is this?" he demanded, trying, as it seemed, to *see* with those sightless eyes—unavailing and distressing attempt! "Answer me—speak again!" he ordered, imperiously and aloud.

"Will you have a little more water, sir? I spilt half of what was in the glass," I said.

"*Who* is it? *What* is it? Who speaks?"

"Pilot knows me, and John and Mary know I am here. I came only this evening," I answered.

"Great God!—what delusion has come over me? What sweet madness has seized me?"

"No delusion—no madness: your mind, sir, is too strong for delusion, your health too sound for frenzy."

"And where is the speaker? Is it only a voice? Oh!

I *cannot* see, but I must feel, or my heart will stop and my brain burst. Whatever—whoever you are—be perceptible to the touch or I cannot live!"

He groped; I arrested his wandering hand, and prisoned it in both mine.

"Her very fingers!" he cried; "her small, slight fingers! If so there must be more of her."

The muscular hand broke from my custody; my arm was seized, my shoulder—neck—waist—I was entwined and gathered to him.

"Is it Jane? *What* is it? This is her shape—this is her size——"

"And this her voice," I added. "She is all here: her heart, too. God bless you, sir! I am glad to be so near you again."

"Jane Eyre!—Jane Eyre," was all he said.

THE CHURCH MILITANT

from *Shirley*.

OF late years an abundant shower of curates has fallen upon the North of England: they lie very thick on the hills; every parish has one or more of them; they are young enough to be very active, and ought to be doing a great deal of good. But not of late years are we about to speak. We are going back to the beginning of this century: late years—present years—are dusty, sunburnt, hot, arid. We will evade the noon—forget it in siesta, pass the mid-day in slumber—and dream of dawn.

If you think, from this prelude, that anything like a romance is preparing for you, reader, you never were more mistaken. Do you anticipate sentiment, and poetry, and reverie? Do you expect passion, and stimulus, and melodrama? Calm your expectations; reduce them to a lowly standard. Something real, cool, and solid lies before you; something unromantic as Monday morning, when all who have work wake with the consciousness that they must rise and betake themselves thereto. It is not positively affirmed that you shall not have a taste of the exciting—perhaps towards the middle and close of the meal—but it is resolved that the first dish set upon the table shall be one that a Catholic—ay, even an Anglo-Catholic—might eat on Good Friday in Passion Week. It shall be cold lentils and vinegar without oil; it shall be unleavened bread with bitter herbs, and no roast lamb.

Of late years, I say, an abundant shower of curates has fallen upon the North of England; but in eighteen-hundred-eleven-twelve that affluent rain had not descended. Curates were scarce then: there was no Pastoral Aid, no Additional Curates' Society to stretch a helping hand to worn-out old rectors and incumbents, and give them the wherewithal to pay a vigorous young colleague from Oxford or Cambridge. The present successors of the Apostles, disciples of Dr Pusey and tools of the Propaganda, were at that time being hatched under cradle-blankets or undergoing regeneration by nursery-baptism in wash-hand basins. You could not have guessed by looking at any one of them that the Italian-ironed double frills of its net-cap surrounded the brows of a pre-ordained, specially sanctified successor of St Paul, St Peter, or St John; nor could you have foreseen in the folds of its long nightgown the white surplice in which it was hereafter cruelly to exercise the souls of its parishioners, and strangely to non-plus its old-fashioned vicar by flourishing aloft in a pulpit the shirt-like raiment which had never before waved higher than the reading-desk.

Yet even in those days of scarcity there were curates: the precious plant was rare, but it might be found. A certain favoured district in the West Riding of Yorkshire could boast three rods of Aaron blossoming within a circuit of twenty miles. You shall see them, reader. Step into this neat garden-house on the skirts of Whinbury, walk forward into the little parlour—there they are at dinner. Allow me to introduce them to you: Mr Donne, curate of Whinbury; Mr Malone, curate of Briarfield; Mr Sweeting, curate of Nunnely. These are Mr Donne's lodgings, being the habitation of one John Gale, a small clothier. Mr Donne has kindly invited his brethren to regale with him. You and I will join the party, see what is to be seen, and hear what is to be heard. At present, however, they are only eating, and while they eat we will talk aside.

These gentlemen are in the bloom of youth: they possess all the activity of that interesting age—an activity which their moping old vicars would fain turn into the channel of their pastoral duties, often expressing a wish to see it expended in a diligent superintendence of the schools, and in frequent visits to the sick of their respective parishes. But the youthful Levites feel this to be dull work; they prefer lavishing their energies on a course of proceeding which—though to other eyes it appear more heavy with ennui, more cursed with monotony, than the toil of the weaver at his loom—seems to yield them an unfailing supply of enjoyment and occupation.

I allude to a rushing backwards and forwards, amongst themselves, to and from their respective lodgings—not a round, but a triangle of visits, which they keep up all the year through, in winter, spring, summer and autumn. Season and weather make no difference; with unintelligible zeal they dare snow and hail, wind and rain, mire and dust, to go and dine or drink tea or sup with each other. What attracts them it would be difficult to say. It is not friendship, for whenever they meet they quarrel. It is not religion; the thing is never named amongst them: theology they may discuss occasionally, but piety—never. It is not the love of eating and drinking; each might have as good a joint and pudding, tea as potent, and toast as succulent, at his own lodgings as is served to him at his brother's. Mrs Gale, Mrs Hogg, and Mrs Whipp—their respective landladies—affirm that "it is just for nought else but to give folk trouble." By "folk" the good ladies of course mean themselves, for indeed they are kept in a continual "fry" by this system of mutual invasion.

Mr Donne and his guests, as I have said, are at dinner; Mrs Gale waits on them, but a spark of the hot kitchen fire is in her eye. She considers that the privilege of inviting a friend to a meal occasionally, without additional charge (a privilege included in the terms on which she lets her lodgings), has been quite sufficiently exercised of late. The present week is yet but at Thursday, and on Monday Mr Malone, the curate of Briarfield, came to breakfast and stayed to dinner; on Tuesday, Mr Malone and Mr Sweeting, of Nunnely, came to tea, remained to supper, occupied the spare bed, and favoured her with their company to breakfast on Wednesday morning; now, on Thursday, they are both here at dinner, and she is almost certain they will stay all night. "C'en est trop," she would say, if she could speak French.

Mr Sweeting is mincing the slice of roast-beef on his plate, and complaining that it is very tough; Mr Donne says the beer is flat. Ay! that is the worst of it: if they would only be civil, Mrs Gale wouldn't mind it so much; if they would only seem satisfied with what they get, she wouldn't care, but "these young persons is so high and so scornful, they set everybody beneath their 'fit': they treat her with less than civility, just because she doesn't keep a servant, but does the work of the house herself, as her mother did afore her: then they are always speaking against Yorkshire ways and Yorkshire folk," and by that very token Mrs Gale does not believe one of them to be a real gentleman, or come of gentle kin. "The old parsons is worth the whole lump of college lads; they know what belongs to good manners, and is kind to high and low."

"More bread!" cries Mr Malone, in a tone which, though prolonged but to utter two syllables, proclaims him at once a native of the land of shamrocks and potatoes. Mrs Gale hates Mr Malone more than either of the other two; but she fears him also, for he is a tall, strongly-built personage, with real Irish legs and arms, and a face as genuinely national: not the Milesian face —not Daniel O'Connell's style, but the high-featured, North-American-Indian sort of visage, which belongs to a certain class of the Irish gentry, and has a petrified and proud look, better suited to the owner of an estate of slaves than to the landlord of a free peasantry. Mr Malone's father termed himself a gentleman; he was poor and in debt, and besottedly arrogant; and his son was like him.

Mrs Gale offered the loaf.

"Cut it, woman," said her guest; and the "woman" cut it accordingly. Had she followed her inclinations, she would have cut the parson also; her Yorkshire soul revolted absolutely from his manner of command.

The curates had good appetites, and though the beef was "tough," they ate a great deal of it. They swallowed, too, a tolerable allowance of the "flat beer," while a dish of Yorkshire pudding, and two tureens of vegetables, disappeared like leaves before locusts. The cheese, too, received distinguished marks of their attention; and a "spice-cake," which followed by way of dessert, vanished like a vision, and was no more found. Its elegy was chanted in the kitchen by Abraham, Mrs Gale's son and heir, a youth of six summers; he had reckoned upon the reversion thereof, and when his mother brought down the empty platter, he lifted up his voice and wept sore.

The curates meantime sat and sipped their wine, a liquor of unpretending vintage, moderately enjoyed. Mr Malone, indeed, would much rather have had whisky; but Mr Donne, being an Englishman, did not keep the beverage. While they sipped they argued; not on politics, nor on philosophy, nor on literature—these topics were now as ever totally without interest for them— not even on theology, practical or doctrinal, but on minute points of ecclesiastical discipline, frivolities which seemed empty as bubbles to all save themselves. Mr Malone, who contrived to secure two glasses of wine when his brethren contented themselves with one, waxed by degrees hilarious after his fashion; that is, he grew a little insolent, said rude things in a hectoring tone, and laughed clamorously at his own brilliancy.

Each of his companions became in turn his butt. Malone had a stock of jokes at their service, which he was accustomed to serve out regularly on convivial occasions like the present, seldom varying his wit, for which, indeed, there was no necessity, as he never appeared to consider himself monotonous, and did not at all care what others thought. Mr Donne he favoured with hints about his extreme meagreness, allusions to his turned-up nose, cutting sarcasms on a certain thread-bare chocolate surtout, which that gentleman was accustomed to sport whenever it rained or seemed likely to rain, and criticisms on a choice set of cockney phrases and modes of pronunciation, Mr Donne's own property, and certainly deserving of remark for the elegance and finish they communicated to his style.

Mr Sweeting was bantered about his stature—he was a little man, a mere boy in height and breadth compared with the athletic Malone—rallied on his musical accomplishments—he played the flute and sang hymns like a seraph (some young ladies of his parish thought), sneered at as "the ladies' pet," teased about his mamma and sisters, for whom poor Mr Sweeting had some lingering regard, and of whom he was foolish enough now and then to speak in the presence of the priestly Paddy, from whose anatomy the bowels of natural affection had somehow been omitted.

The victims met these attacks each in his own way;

Mr Donne with a stilted self-complacency, and half-sullen phlegm, the sole props of his otherwise somewhat rickety dignity; Mr Sweeting with the indifference of a light, easy disposition, which never professed to have any dignity to maintain.

When Malone's raillery became rather too offensive, which it soon did, they joined in an attempt to turn the tables on him by asking him how many boys had shouted "Irish Peter!" after him as he came along the road that day (Malone's name was Peter—the Rev. Peter Augustus Malone); requesting to be informed whether it was the mode in Ireland for clergymen to carry loaded pistols in their pockets, and a shillelagh in their hands, when they made pastoral visits; inquiring the signification of such words as vele, firrum, hellum, storrum (so Mr Malone invariably pronounced veil, firm, helm, storm), and employing such other methods of retaliation as the innate refinement of their minds suggested.

This, of course, would not do. Malone, being neither good-natured nor phlegmatic, was presently in a towering passion. He vociferated, gesticulated; Donne and Sweeting laughed. He reviled them as Saxons and snobs at the very top pitch of his high Celtic voice; they taunted him with being the native of a conquered land. He menaced rebellion in the name of his "counthry," vented bitter hatred against English rule; they spoke of rags, beggary, and pestilence. The little parlour was in an uproar; you would have thought a duel must follow such virulent abuse; it seemed a wonder that Mr and Mrs Gale did not take alarm at the noise, and send for a constable to keep the peace. But they were accustomed to such demonstrations; they well knew that the curates never dined or took tea together without a little exercise of the sort, and were quite easy as to consequences; knowing that these clerical quarrels were as harmless as they were noisy; that they resulted in nothing, and that, on whatever terms the curates might part to-night, they would be sure to meet the best friends in the world to-morrow morning.

As the worthy pair were sitting by their kitchen-fire, listening to the repeated and sonorous contact of Malone's fist with the mahogany plane of the parlour-table, and to the consequent start and jingle of decanters and glasses following each assault, to the mocking laughter of the allied English disputants, and the stuttering declamation of the isolated Hibernian—as they thus sat a foot was heard at the outer door-step, and the knocker quivered to a sharp appeal.

Mr Gale went and opened.

"Whom have you upstairs in the parlour?" asked a voice—a rather remarkable voice, nasal in tone, abrupt in utterance.

"Oh! Mr Helstone, is it you, sir? I could hardly see you for the darkness; it is so soon dark now. Will you walk in, sir?"

"I want to know first whether it is worth my while walking in. Whom have you upstairs?"

"The curates, sir."

"What! all of them?"

"Yes, sir."

"Been dining here?"

"Yes, sir."

"That will do."

With these words a person entered—a middle-aged man, in black. He walked straight across the kitchen to an inner door, opened it, inclined his head forward, and stood listening. There was something to listen to, for the noise above was just then louder than ever.

"Hey!" he ejaculated to himself; then turning to Mr Gale: "Have you often this sort of work?"

Mr Gale had been a churchwarden, and was indulgent to the clergy.

"They're young, you know, sir—they're young," said he deprecatingly.

"Young! They want caning. Bad boys—bad boys. And if you were a Dissenter, John Gale, instead of being a good Churchman, they'd do the like—they'd expose themselves; but I'll——"

By way of finish to this sentence, he passed through the inner door, drew it after him, and mounted the stair. Again he listened a few minutes when he arrived at the upper room. Making entrance without warning, he stood before the curates.

And they were silent; they were transfixed; and so was the invader. He—a personage short of stature, but straight of port, and bearing on broad shoulders a hawk's head, beak, and eye, the whole surmounted by a Rehoboam, or shovel hat, which he did not seem to think it necessary to lift or remove before the presence in which he then stood—*he* folded his arms on his chest and surveyed his young friends—if friends they were—much at his leisure.

"What!" he began, delivering his words in a voice no longer nasal, but deep—more than deep—a voice made purposely hollow and cavernous—"what! has the miracle of Pentecost been renewed? Have the cloven tongues come down again? Where are they? The sound filled the whole house just now. I heard the seventeen languages in full action: Parthians, and Medes, and Elamites, the dwellers in Mesopotamia, and in Judæa, and Cappadocia, in Pontus and Asia, Phrygia and Pamphylia, in Egypt and in the parts of Libya about Cyrene, strangers of Rome, Jews and proselytes, Cretes and Arabians—every one of these must have had its representative in this room two minutes since."

"I beg your pardon, Mr Helstone," began Mr Donne; "take a seat, pray, sir. Have a glass of wine?"

His civilities received no answer. The falcon in the black coat proceeded:

"What do I talk about the gift of tongues? Gift, indeed! I mistook the chapter, and book, and testament:

Gospel for law, Acts for Genesis, the city of Jerusalem for the plain of Shinar. It was no gift, but the confusion of tongues which has gabbled me deaf as a post. *You* apostles? What? you three? Certainly not. Three presumptuous Babylonish masons—neither more nor less!"

"I assure you, sir, we were only having a little chat together over a glass of wine after a friendly dinner—settling the Dissenters."

"Oh! settling the Dissenters, were you? Was Malone settling the Dissenters? It sounded to me much more like settling his co-apostles. You were quarrelling together, making almost as much noise—you three alone —as Moses Barraclough, the preaching tailor, and all his hearers, are making in the Methodist Chapel down yonder, where they are in the thick of a revival. I know whose fault it is—it is yours, Malone."

"Mine, sir?"

"Yours, sir. Donne and Sweeting were quiet before you came, and would be quiet if you were gone. I wish when you crossed the Channel you had left your Irish habits behind you. Dublin student ways won't do here; the proceedings which might pass unnoticed in a wild bog and mountain district in Connaught will, in a decent English parish, bring disgrace on those who indulge in them, and, what is far worse, on the sacred institution of which they are merely the humble appendages."

There was a certain dignity in the little elderly gentleman's manner of rebuking these youths, though it was not, perhaps, quite the dignity most appropriate to the occasion. Mr Helstone, standing straight as a ramrod, looking keen as a kite, presented, despite his clerical hat, black coat, and gaiters, more the air of a veteran officer chiding his subalterns than of a venerable priest exhorting his sons in the faith. Gospel mildness, apostolic benignity, never seemed to have breathed their influence over that keen brown visage; but firmness had fixed the features, and sagacity had carved her own lines about them.

"I met Supplehough," he continued, "plodding through the mud this wet night, going to preach at Milldean opposition shop. As I told you, I heard Barraclough bellowing in the midst of a conventicle like a possessed bull; and I find *you*, gentlemen, tarrying over your half-pint of muddy port wine, and scolding like angry old women. No wonder Supplehough should have dipped sixteen adult converts in a day, which he did a fortnight since; no wonder Barraclough, scamp and hypocrite as he is, should attract all the weaver girls, in their flowers and ribbons, to witness how much harder are his knuckles than the wooden brim of his tub; as little wonder that *you*, when you are left to yourselves, without your Rectors—myself, and Hall, and Boultby—to back you, should too often perform the holy service of our Church to bare walls, and read your bit of dry discourse to the clerk, and the organist, and the beadle. But enough of the subject. I came to see Malone. I have an errand unto thee, O captain!"

"What is it?" inquired Malone discontentedly. "There can be no funeral to take at this time of day."

"Have you any arms about you?"

"Arms, sir? Yes, and legs"; and he advanced the mighty members.

"Bah! weapons, I mean."

"I have the pistols you gave me yourself; I never part with them; I lay them ready cocked on a chair by my bedside at night. I have my blackthorn."

"Very good. Will you go to Hollow's Mill?"

"What is stirring at Hollow's Mill?"

"Nothing as yet, nor perhaps will be; but Moore is alone there: he has sent all the workmen he can trust to Stilbro'; there are only two women left about the place. It would be a nice opportunity for any of his well-wishers to pay him a visit, if they only knew how straight the path was made before them."

"I am none of his well-wishers, sir: I don't care for him."

"Soh! Malone, you are afraid."

"You know me better than that. If I really thought there was a chance of a row, I would go; but Moore is a strange, shy man, whom I never pretend to understand; and, for the sake of his sweet company only, I would not stir a step."

"But there *is* a chance of a row; if a positive riot does not take place—of which, indeed, I see no signs—yet it is unlikely this night will pass quite tranquilly. You know Moore has resolved to have the new machinery, and he expects two waggon-loads of frames and shears from Stilbro' this evening. Scott, the overlooker, and a few picked men, are gone to fetch them."

"They will bring them in safely and quietly enough, sir."

"Moore says so, and affirms he wants nobody: someone, however, he must have, if it were only to bear evidence in case anything should happen. I call him very careless. He sits in the counting-house with the shutters unclosed; he goes out here and there after dark, wanders right up the hollow, down Fieldhead Lane, among the plantations, just as if he were the darling of the neighbourhood, or —being, as he is, its detestation—bore a 'charmed life,' as they say in tale-books. He takes no warning from the fate of Pearson, nor from that of Armitage—shot, one in his own house and the other on the moor."

"But he should take warning, sir, and use precautions too," interposed Mr Sweeting; "and I think he would if he heard what I heard the other day."

"What did you hear, Davy?"

"You know Mike Hartley, sir?"

"The Antinomian weaver. Yes."

"When Mike has been drinking for a few weeks together, he generally winds up by a visit to Nunnely Vicarage, to tell Mr Hall a piece of his mind about his sermons, to denounce the horrible tendency of his doctrine of works, and warn him that he and all his hearers are sitting in outer darkness."

"Well, that has nothing to do with Moore."

"Besides being an Antinomian, he is a violent Jacobin and leveller, sir."

"I know. When he is very drunk, his mind is always running on regicide. Mike is not unacquainted with history, and it is rich to hear him going over the list of tyrants of whom, as he says, 'the revenger of blood has obtained satisfaction.' The fellow exults strangely in murder done on crowned heads, or on any head for political reasons. I have already heard it hinted that he seems to have a queer hankering after Moore: is that what you allude to, Sweeting?"

"You use the proper term, sir. Mr Hall thinks Mike has no personal hatred of Moore; Mike says he even likes to talk to him, and run after him, but he has a *hankering* that Moore should be made an example of. He was extolling him to Mr Hall the other day as the mill-owner with the most brains in Yorkshire, and for that reason he affirms Moore should be chosen as a sacrifice, an oblation of a sweet savour. Is Mike Hartley in his right mind, do you think, sir?" inquired Sweeting simply.

"Can't tell, Davy: he may be crazed or he may be only crafty—or, perhaps, a little of both."

"He talks of seeing visions, sir."

"Ay! He is a very Ezekiel or Daniel for visions. He came just when I was going to bed, last Friday night, to describe one that had been revealed to him in Nunnely Park that very afternoon."

"Tell it, sir—what was it?" urged Sweeting.

"Davy, thou hast an enormous organ of Wonder in thy cranium; Malone, you see, has none; neither murders nor visions interest him. See what a big vacant Saph he looks at this moment."

"Saph! Who was Saph, sir?"

"I thought you would not know: you may find it out; it is biblical. I know nothing more of him than his name and race; but from a boy upwards I have always attached a personality to Saph. Depend on it he was honest, heavy, and luckless; he met his end at Gob, by the hand of Sibbechai.''

"But the vision, sir?''

"Davy, thou shalt hear. Donne is biting his nails, and Malone yawning; so I will tell it but to thee. Mike is out of work, like many others, unfortunately; Mr Grame, Sir Philip Nunnely's steward, gave him a job about the Priory. According to his account, Mike was busy hedging rather late in the afternoon, but before dark, when he heard what he thought was a band at a distance —bugles, fifes, and the sound of a trumpet; it came from the forest, and he wondered that there should be music there. He looked up: all amongst the trees he saw moving objects, red, like poppies, or white, like May-blossom; the wood was full of them, they poured out and filled the park. He then perceived they were soldiers— thousands and tens of thousands; but they made no more noise than a swarm of midges on a summer evening. They formed in order, he affirmed, and marched, regiment after regiment, across the park; he followed them to Nunnely Common; the music still played soft and distant. On the common he watched them go through a number of evolutions—a man clothed in scarlet stood in the centre and directed them; they extended, he declared, over fifty acres; they were in sight half an hour; then they marched away quite silently; the whole time he heard neither voice nor tread—nothing but the faint music playing a solemn march.''

"Where did they go, sir?''

"Towards Briarfield. Mike followed them; they seemed passing Fieldhead, when a column of smoke, such as might be vomited by a park of artillery, spread noiseless over the fields, the road, the common, and rolled, he said, blue and dim, to his very feet. As it cleared away he looked again for the soldiers, but they were vanished; he saw them no more. Mike, like a wise

Daniel as he is, not only rehearsed the vision, but gave the interpretation thereof: it signifies, he intimated, bloodshed and civil conflict."

"Do you credit it, sir?" asked Sweeting.

"Do you, Davy? But come, Malone, why are you not off?"

"I am rather surprised, sir, you did not stay with Moore yourself; you like this kind of thing."

"So I should have done, had I not unfortunately happened to engage Boultby to sup with me on his way home from the Bible Society meeting at Nunnely. I promised to send you as my substitute, for which, by-the-by, he did not thank me: he would much rather have had me than you, Peter. Should there be any real need of help, I shall join you; the mill-bell will give warning. Meantime, go, unless" (turning suddenly to Messrs Sweeting and Donne)—"unless Davy Sweeting or Joseph Donne prefers going. What do you say, gentlemen? The commission is an honourable one, not without the seasoning of a little real peril; for the country is in a queer state, as you all know, and Moore and his mill and his machinery are held in sufficient odium. There are chivalric sentiments, there is high-beating courage under those waistcoats of yours, I doubt not. Perhaps I am too partial to my favourite, Peter; little David shall be the champion, or spotless Joseph. Malone, you are but a great floundering Saul after all, good only to lend your armour: out with your fire-arms, fetch your shillelagh; it is there—in the corner."

With a significant grin, Malone produced his pistols, offering one to each of his brethren. They were not readily seized on; with graceful modesty each gentleman retired a step from the presented weapon.

"I never touch them; I never did touch anything of the kind," said Mr Donne.

"I am almost a stranger to Mr Moore," murmured Sweeting.

"If you never touched a pistol, try the feel of it now, great satrap of Egypt. As to the little minstrel, he probably prefers encountering the Philistines with no other weapon than his flute. Get their hats, Peter; they'll both of 'em go."

"No, sir; no, Mr Helstone: my mother wouldn't like it," pleaded Sweeting.

"And I make it a rule never to get mixed up in affairs of the kind," observed Donne.

Helstone smiled sardonically; Malone laughed a horse-laugh. He then replaced his arms, took his hat and cudgel, and saying that "he never felt more in tune for a shindy in his life, and that he wished a score of greasy cloth-dressers might beat up Moore's quarters that night," he made his exit, clearing the stairs at a stride or two, and making the house shake with the bang of the front-door behind him.

The evening was pitch-dark: star and moon were quenched in gray rain-clouds—gray they would have been by day, by night they looked sable. Malone was not a man given to close observation of Nature; her changes passed, for the most part, unnoticed by him: he could walk miles on the most varying April day, and never see the beautiful dallying of earth and heaven; never mark when a sunbeam kissed the hill-tops, making them smile clear in green light, or when a shower wept over them, hiding their crests with the low-hanging, dishevelled tresses of a cloud. He did not, therefore, care to contrast the sky as it now appeared—a muffled, steaming vault, all black, save where, towards the east, the furnaces of Stilbro' ironworks threw a tremulous lurid shimmer on the horizon—with the same sky on an unclouded, frosty night. He did not trouble himself to ask where the constellations and the planets were gone, or to regret the "black-blue" serenity of the air-ocean which those white islets stud, and which another ocean of heavier and denser element now rolled below and concealed. He just doggedly pursued his way, leaning a little forward as he walked, and wearing his hat on the back of his head, as his Irish manner was. "Tramp, tramp," he went along the causeway, where the road boasted the privilege of such an accommodation; "splash, splash," through the mire-filled cart-ruts, where the flags were exchanged for soft mud. He looked but for certain land-marks: the spire of Briarfield church; further on, the lights of Redhouse. This was an inn, and when he reached it, the glow of a fire through a half-curtained window, a vision of glasses on a round table, and of revellers on an oaken settle, had nearly drawn aside the curate from his course. He thought longingly of a tumbler of whisky-and-water; in a strange place, he would instantly have realized the dream, but the company assembled in that kitchen were Mr Helstone's own parishioners; they all knew him. He sighed, and passed on.

The high road was now to be quitted, as the remaining distance to Hollow's Mill might be considerably reduced by a short-cut across fields. These fields were level and monotonous: Malone took a direct course through them, jumping hedge and wall. He passed but one building here, and that seemed large and hall-like, though irregular: you could see a high gable, then a long front, then a low gable, then a thick, lofty stack of chimneys: there were some trees behind it. It was dark; not a candle shone from any window; it was absolutely still: the rain running from the eaves, and the rather wild but very low whistle of the wind round the chimneys and through the boughs, were the sole sounds in its neighbourhood.

This building passed, the fields, hitherto flat, declined in a rapid descent; evidently a vale lay below, through which you could hear the water run. One light glimmered in the depth. For that beacon Malone steered.

He came to a little white house—you could see it was white, even through this dense darkness—and knocked

T   9

at the door. A fresh-faced servant opened it. By the candle she held was revealed a narrow passage, terminating in a narrow stair. Two doors, covered with crimson baize, a strip of crimson carpet down the steps, contrasted with light-coloured walls and white floor, made the little interior look clean and fresh.

"Mr Moore is at home, I suppose?"

"Yes, sir, but he is not in."

"Not in! Where is he, then?"

"At the mill, in the counting-house."

Here one of the crimson doors opened.

"Are the waggons come, Sarah?" asked a female voice, and a female head at the same time was apparent.

It might not be the head of a goddess—indeed, a screw of curl-paper on each side of the temples quite forbade that supposition—but neither was it the head of a Gorgon; yet Malone seemed to take it in the latter light. Big as he was, he shrank bashfully back into the rain at the view thereof, and saying, "I'll go to him," hurried in seeming trepidation down a short lane, across an obscure yard, towards a huge black mill.

The work hours were over, the "hands" were gone, the machinery was at rest, the mill shut up. Malone walked round it. Somewhere in its great sooty flank he found another chink of light. He knocked at another door, using for the purpose the thick end of his shillelagh, with which he beat a rousing tattoo. A key turned: the door unclosed.

"Is it Joe Scott? What news of the waggons, Joe?"

"No—it's myself. Mr Helstone would send me."

"Oh! Mr Malone." The voice, in uttering this name, had the slightest possible cadence of disappointment. After a moment's pause it continued politely, but a little formally: "I beg you will come in, Mr Malone. I regret extremely Mr Helstone should have thought it necessary to trouble you so far: there was no necessity—I told him so—and on such a night. But walk forwards."

Through a dark apartment, of aspect undistinguishable, Malone followed the speaker into a light and bright room within—very light and bright indeed it seemed to eyes which, for the last hour, had been striving to penetrate the double darkness of night and fog; but, except for its excellent fire and for a lamp of elegant design and vivid lustre burning on a table, it was a very plain place. The boarded floor was carpetless; the three or four stiff-backed, green-painted chairs seemed once to have furnished the kitchen of some farmhouse; a desk of strong, solid formation, the table aforesaid, and some framed sheets on the stone-coloured walls, bearing plans for building, for gardening, designs of machinery, etc., completed the furniture of the place.

Plain as it was, it seemed to satisfy Malone, who, when he had removed and hung up his wet surtout and hat, drew one of the rheumatic-looking chairs to the hearth, and set his knees almost within the bars of the red grate.

"Comfortable quarters you have here, Mr Moore, and all snug to yourself."

"Yes; but my sister would be glad to see you, if you would prefer stepping into the house."

"Oh no; the ladies are best alone. I never was a lady's man. You don't mistake me for my friend Sweeting, do you, Mr Moore?"

"Sweeting? Which of them is that—the gentleman in the chocolate overcoat, or the little gentleman?"

"The little one—he of Nunnely, the cavalier of the Misses Sykes, with the whole six of whom he is in love. Ha! ha!"

"Better be generally in love with all than specially with one, I should think, in that quarter."

"But he *is* specially in love with one besides, for when I and Donne urged him to make a choice amongst the fair bevy, he named—which do you think?"

With a queer, quiet smile Mr Moore replied:

"Dora, of course, or Harriet."

"Ha! ha! you've an excellent guess. But what made you hit on those two?"

"Because they are the tallest, the handsomest, and Dora, at least, is the stoutest; and as your friend Mr Sweeting is but a little slight figure, I concluded that, according to a frequent rule in such cases, he preferred his contrast."

"You are right: Dora it is. But he has no chance, has he, Moore?"

"What has Mr Sweeting besides his curacy?"

This question seemed to tickle Malone amazingly. He laughed for full three minutes before he answered it.

"What has Sweeting? Why, David has his harp, or flute, which comes to the same thing. He has a sort of pinchbeck watch; ditto, ring; ditto, eyeglass—that's what he has."

"How would he propose to keep Miss Sykes in gowns only?"

"Ha! ha! excellent! I'll ask him that next time I see him. I'll roast him for his presumption. But no doubt he expects old Christopher Sykes would do something handsome. He is rich, is he not? They live in a large house."

"Sykes carries on an extensive concern."

"Therefore he must be wealthy, eh?"

"Therefore he must have plenty to do with his wealth, and in these times would be about as likely to think of drawing money from the business to give dowries to his daughters as I should be to dream of pulling down the cottage there, and constructing on its ruins a house as large as Fieldhead."

"Do you know what I heard, Moore, the other day?"

"No; perhaps that I *was* about to effect some such change. Your Briarfield gossips are capable of saying that or sillier things."

"That you were going to take Fieldhead on a lease—I thought it looked a dismal place, by-the-by, to-night

as I passed it—and that it was your intention to settle
a Miss Sykes there as mistress—to be married, in short.
Ha! ha! Now, which is it? Dora, I am sure; you said
she was the handsomest."

"I wonder how often it has been settled that I was
to be married since I came to Briarfield! They have
assigned me every marriageable single woman by turns
in the district. Now it was the two Misses Wynns—first
the dark, then the light one; now the red-haired Miss
Armitage, then the mature Ann Pearson; at present you
throw on my shoulders all the tribe of the Misses Sykes.
On what grounds this gossip rests God knows. I visit
nowhere: I seek female society about as assiduously as
you do, Mr Malone. If ever I go to Whinbury, it is only
to give Sykes or Pearson a call in their counting-house,
where our discussions run on other topics than matrimony, and our thoughts are occupied with other things
than courtships, establishments, dowries—the cloth we
can't sell, the hands we can't employ, the mills we can't
run, the perverse course of events generally which we
cannot alter, fill our hearts, I take it, pretty well at
present, to the tolerably complete exclusion of such
figments as love-making, etc."

"I go along with you completely, Moore. If there is one
notion I hate more than another, it is that of marriage—
I mean marriage in the vulgar, weak sense, as a mere
matter of sentiment: two beggarly fools agreeing to
unite their indigence by some fantastic tie of feeling.
Humbug! But an advantageous connection, such as
can be formed in consonance with dignity of views and
permanency of solid interests, is not so bad, eh?"

"No," responded Moore, in an absent manner.

The subject seemed to have no interest for him; he did
not pursue it. After sitting for some time gazing at the
fire with a preoccupied air, he suddenly turned his
head.

"Hark!" said he. "Did you hear wheels?"

Rising, he went to the window, opened it, and listened. He soon closed it.

"It is only the sound of the wind rising," he remarked, "and the rivulet a little swollen rushing down the hollow. I expected those waggons at six; it is near nine now."

"Seriously, do you suppose that the putting up of this new machinery will bring you into danger?" inquired Malone. "Helstone seems to think it will."

"I only wish the machines—the frames—were safe here, and lodged within the walls of this mill. Once put up, I defy the frame-breakers. Let them only pay me a visit, and take the consequences; my mill is my castle."

"One despises such low scoundrels," observed Malone, in a profound vein of reflection. "I almost wish a party would call upon you to-night; but the road seemed extremely quiet as I came along: I saw nothing astir."

"You came by the Redhouse?"

"Yes."

"There would be nothing on that road; it is in the direction of Stilbro' the risk lies."

"And you think there is risk?"

"What these fellows have done to others, they may do to me. There is only this difference: most of the manufacturers seem paralyzed when they are attacked. Sykes, for instance, when his dressing-shop was set on fire and burned to the ground, when the cloth was torn from his tenters and left in shreds in the field, took no steps to discover or punish the miscreants: he gave up as tamely as a rabbit under the jaws of a ferret. Now I, if I know myself, should stand by my trade, my mill, and my machinery."

"Helstone says these three are your gods; that the 'Orders in Council' are with you another name for the seven deadly sins; that Castlereagh is your Antichrist, and the war-party his legions."

"Yes; I abhor all these things because they ruin me; they stand in my way; I cannot get on. I cannot execute my plans because of them; I see myself baffled at every turn by their untoward effects."

"But you are rich and thriving, Moore?"

"I am very rich in cloth I cannot sell: you should step into my warehouse yonder, and observe how it is piled to the roof with pieces. Roakes and Pearson are in the same condition. America used to be their market, but the Orders in Council have cut them off."

Malone did not seem prepared to carry on briskly a conversation of this sort; he began to knock the heels of his boots together, and to yawn.

"And then to think," continued Mr Moore, who seemed too much taken up with the current of his own thoughts to note the symptoms of his guest's ennui—"to think that these ridiculous gossips of Whinbury and Briarfield will keep pestering one about being married! As if there was nothing to be done in life but to 'pay attention,' as they say, to some young lady, and then to go to church with her, and then to start on a bridal tour, and then to run through a round of visits, and then, I suppose, to be 'having a family.'—Oh, que le diable emporte!"—He broke off the aspiration into which he was launching with a certain energy, and added, more calmly: "I believe women talk and think only of these things, and they naturally fancy men's minds similarly occupied."

"Of course—of course," assented Malone; "but never mind them." And he whistled, looked impatiently round, and seemed to feel a great want of something. This time Moore caught, and, it appeared, comprehended his demonstrations.

"Mr Malone," said he, "you must require refreshment after your wet walk; I forget hospitality."

"Not at all," rejoined Malone; but he looked as if the right nail was at last hit on the head, nevertheless. Moore rose and opened a cupboard.

"It is my fancy," said he, "to have every convenience

within myself, and not to be dependent on the feminity in the cottage yonder for every mouthful I eat or every drop I drink. I often spend the evening and sup here alone, and sleep with Joe Scott in the mill. Sometimes I am my own watchman; I require little sleep, and it pleases me on a fine night to wander for an hour or two with my musket about the hollow. Mr Malone, can you cook a mutton-chop?"

"Try me: I've done it hundreds of times at college."

"There's a dishful, then, and there's the gridiron. Turn them quickly; you know the secret of keeping the juices in?"

"Never fear me—you shall see. Hand a knife and fork, please."

The curate turned up his coat-cuffs, and applied himself to the cookery with vigour. The manufacturer placed on the table plates, a loaf of bread, a black bottle, and two tumblers. He then produced a small copper kettle —still from the same well-stored recess, his cupboard— filled it with water from a large stone jar in a corner, set it on the fire beside the hissing gridiron, got lemons, sugar, and a small china punch-bowl; but while he was brewing the punch a tap at the door called him away.

"Is it you, Sarah?"

"Yes, sir. Will you come to supper, please, sir?"

"No; I shall not be in to-night. I shall sleep in the mill. So lock the doors, and tell your mistress to go to bed."

He returned.

"You have your household in proper order," observed Malone approvingly, as, with his fine face ruddy as the embers over which he bent, he assiduously turned the mutton-chops. "You are not under petticoat government, like poor Sweeting; a man—whew!—how the fat spits!—it has burnt my hand—destined to be ruled by women. Now, you and I, Moore—there's a fine brown one for you, and full of gravy—you and I will have no gray mares in our stables when we marry."

"I don't know—I never think about it: if the gray mare is handsome and tractable, why not?"

"The chops are done; is the punch brewed?"

"There is a glassful; taste it. When Joe Scott and his minions return they shall have a share of this, provided they bring home the frames intact."

Malone waxed very exultant over the supper; he laughed aloud at trifles, made bad jokes and applauded them himself, and, in short, grew unmeaningly noisy. His host, on the contrary, remained quiet as before. It is time, reader, that you should have some idea of the appearance of this same host; I must endeavour to sketch him as he sits at table.

He is what you would probably call at first view rather a strange-looking man, for he is thin, dark, sallow, very foreign of aspect, with shadowy hair carelessly streaking his forehead; it appears that he spends but little time at his toilette, or he would arrange it with more taste. He seems unconscious that his features are fine, that they have a Southern symmetry, clearness, regularity in their chiselling; nor does a spectator become aware of this advantage till he has examined him well, for an anxious countenance and a hollow, somewhat haggard, outline of face, disturb the idea of beauty with one of care. His eyes are large, and grave, and gray; their expression is intent and meditative, rather searching than soft, rather thoughtful than genial. When he parts his lips in a smile his physiognomy is agreeable—not that it is frank or cheerful even then, but you feel the influence of a certain sedate charm, suggestive, whether truly or delusively, of a considerate, perhaps a kind nature; of feelings that may wear well at home; patient, forbearing, possibly faithful feelings. He is still young—not more than thirty; his stature is tall, his figure slender. His manner of speaking displeases; he has an outlandish accent, which, notwithstanding a studied carelessness of pronunciation and diction, grates on a British, and especially on a Yorkshire ear.

Mr Moore, indeed, was but half a Briton, and scarcely that. He came of a foreign ancestry by the mother's side, and was himself born and partly reared on a foreign soil. A hybrid in nature, it is probable he had a hybrid's feeling on many points—patriotism for one; it is likely that he was unapt to attach himself to parties, to sects, even to climes and customs; it is not impossible that he had a tendency to isolate his individual person from any community amidst which his lot might temporarily happen to be thrown, and that he felt it to be his best wisdom to push the interests of Robert Gérard Moore, to the exclusion of philanthropic consideration for general interest, with which he regarded the said Gérard Moore as in a great measure disconnected. Trade was Mr Moore's hereditary calling—the Gérards of Antwerp had been merchants for two centuries back. Once they had been wealthy merchants, but the uncertainties, the involvements of business had come upon them; disastrous speculations had loosened by degrees the foundations of their credit; the house had stood on a tottering base for a dozen years; and at last, in the shock of the French Revolution, it had rushed down a total ruin. In its fall was involved the English and Yorkshire firm of Moore, closely connected with the Antwerp house, and of which one of the partners resident in Antwerp, Robert Moore, had married Hortense Gérard, with the prospect of his bride inheriting her father Constantine Gérard's share in the business. She inherited, as we have seen, but his share in the liabilities of the firm, and these liabilities, though duly set aside by a composition with creditors, some said her son Robert accepted, in his turn, as a legacy, and that he aspired one day to discharge them, and to rebuild the fallen house of Gérard and Moore on a scale at least equal to its former greatness. It was even supposed that he took by-past circumstances much to heart, and if a childhood passed at the side of a saturnine mother, under foreboding of coming evil, and a manhood drenched and blighted by the pitiless descent of the storm, could painfully impress the mind, *his* probably was impressed in no golden characters.

If, however, he had a great end of restoration in view, it was not in his power to employ great means for its attainment; he was obliged to be content with the day of small things. When he came to Yorkshire, he—whose ancestors had owned warehouses in this seaport, and factories in that inland town, had possessed their town-house and their country-seat—saw no way open to him but to rent a cloth-mill, in an out-of-the-way nook of an out-of-the-way district; to take a cottage adjoining it for his residence, and to add to his possessions, as pasture for his horse and space for his cloth-tenters, a few acres of the steep rugged land that lined the hollow through which his mill-stream brawled. All this he held at a somewhat high rent (for these war times were hard, and everything was dear), of the trustees of the Fieldhead estate, then the property of a minor.

At the time this history commences, Robert Moore had lived but two years in the district, during which period he had at least proved himself possessed of the quality of activity. The dingy cottage was converted into a neat tasteful residence. Of part of the rough land he had made garden-ground, which he cultivated with singular, even with Flemish, exactness and care. As to the mill, which was an old structure and fitted up with old machinery now become inefficient and out of date, he had from the first evinced the strongest contempt for all its arrangements and appointments; his aim had been to effect a radical reform, which he had executed as fast as his very limited capital would allow; and the narrow-ness of that capital, and consequent check on his progress, was a restraint which galled his spirit sorely. Moore ever wanted to push on: "Forward" was the device stamped upon his soul; but poverty curbed him; sometimes (figuratively) he foamed at the mouth when the reins were drawn very tight.

In this state of feeling, it is not to be expected that he would deliberate much as to whether his advance was or was not prejudicial to others. Not being a native, nor for any length of time a resident of the neighbourhood, he did not sufficiently care when the new inventions threw the old workpeople out of employ: he never asked himself where those to whom he no longer paid weekly wages found daily bread, and in this negligence he only resembled thousands besides, on whom the starving poor of Yorkshire seemed to have a closer claim.

The period of which I write was an overshadowed one in British history, and especially in the history of the northern provinces. War was then at its height. Europe was all involved therein. England, if not weary, was worn with long resistance—yes, and half her people were weary, too, and cried out for peace on any terms. National honour was become a mere empty name, of no value in the eyes of many, because their sight was dim with famine; and for a morsel of meat they would have sold their birthright.

The "Orders in Council," provoked by Napoleon's Milan and Berlin decrees, and forbidding neutral Powers to trade with France, had, by offending America, cut off the principal market of the Yorkshire woollen trade, and brought it, consequently, to the verge of ruin. Minor foreign markets were glutted, and would receive no more —the Brazils, Portugal, Sicily were all overstocked by nearly two years' consumption. At this crisis certain inventions in machinery were introduced into the staple manufactures of the North, which, greatly reducing the number of hands necessary to be employed, threw thousands out of work, and left them without legitimate means of sustaining life. A bad harvest supervened.

Distress reached its climax. Endurance, overgoaded, stretched the hand of fraternity to sedition. The throes of a sort of moral earthquake were felt heaving under the hills of the northern counties. But, as is usual in such cases, nobody took much notice. When a food-riot broke out in a manufacturing town, when a gig-mill was burnt to the ground, or a manufacturer's house was attacked, the furniture thrown into the streets, and the family forced to flee for their lives, some local measures were or were not taken by the local magistracy: a ringleader was detected, or more frequently suffered to elude detection; newspaper paragraphs were written on the subject, and there the thing stopped. As to the sufferers, whose sole inheritance was labour, and who had lost that inheritance—who could not get work, and consequently could not get wages, and consequently could not get bread—they were left to suffer on, perhaps inevitably left: it would not do to stop the progress of invention, to damage science, by discouraging its improvements. The war could not be terminated, efficient relief could not be raised—there was no help then—so the unemployed underwent their destiny: ate the bread and drank the waters of affliction.

Misery generates hate. These sufferers hated the machines which they believed took their bread from them; they hated the buildings which contained those machines; they hated the manufacturers who owned those buildings. In the parish of Briarfield, with which we have at present to do, Hollow's Mill was the place held most abominable; Gérard Moore, in his double character of semi-foreigner and thoroughgoing progressist, the man most abominated. And it perhaps rather agreed with Moore's temperament than otherwise to be generally hated, especially when he believed the thing for which he was hated a right and an expedient thing, and it was with a sense of warlike excitement he, on this night, sat in his counting-house waiting the arrival of his frame-laden waggons. Malone's coming and company were, it may be, most unwelcome to him: he would have preferred sitting alone, for he liked a silent, sombre, unsafe solitude. His watchman's musket would have been company enough for him; the full-flowing beck in the den would have delivered continuously the discourse most genial to his ear.

With the queerest look in the world had the manufacturer for some ten minutes been watching the Irish curate, as the latter made free with the punch, when suddenly that steady gray eye changed, as if another vision came between it and Malone. Moore raised his hand.

"Chut!" he said in his French fashion as Malone made a noise with his glass. He listened a moment, then rose, put his hat on, and went out at the counting-house door.

The night was still, dark, and stagnant; the water yet rushed on full and fast; its flow almost seemed a flood in the utter silence. Moore's ear, however, caught another sound—very distant, but yet dissimilar—broken and rugged—in short, a sound of heavy wheels crunching a stony road. He returned to the counting-house and lit a lantern, with which he walked down the mill-yard, and proceeded to open the gates. The big waggons were coming on; the dray-horses' huge hoofs were heard splashing in the mud and water. Moore hailed them:

"Hey, Joe Scott! Is all right?"

Probably Joe Scott was yet at too great a distance to hear the inquiry; he did not answer it.

"Is all right? I say," again asked Moore, when the elephant-like leader's nose almost touched his.

Someone jumped out from the foremost waggon into the road; a voice cried aloud:

"Ay, ay, divil, all's raight. We've smashed 'em."

And there was a run. The waggons stood still; they were now deserted.

"Joe Scott!" No Joe Scott answered. "Murgatroyd!
Pighills! Sykes!" No reply. Mr Moore lifted his lantern
and looked into the vehicles. There was neither man nor
machinery; they were empty and abandoned.

Now, Mr Moore loved his machinery; he had risked
the last of his capital on the purchase of these frames and
shears which to-night had been expected; speculations
most important to his interests depended on the results
to be wrought by them. Where were they?

The words, "We've smashed 'em!" rang in his ears.
How did the catastrophe affect him? By the light of the
lantern he held his features were visible, relaxing to a
singular smile—the smile the man of determined spirit
wears when he reaches a juncture in his life where this
determined spirit is to feel a demand on its strength, when
the strain is to be made, and the faculty must bear or
break. Yet he remained silent, and even motionless, for
at the instant he neither knew what to say nor what to
do. He placed the lantern on the ground, and stood with
his arms folded, gazing down and reflecting.

An impatient trampling of one of the horses made him
presently look up; his eye in the moment caught the
gleam of something white attached to a part of the harness.
Examined by the light of the lantern, this proved to be
a folded paper—a billet. It bore no address without;
within was the superscription:

"To the Divil of Hollow's Miln."

We will not copy the rest of the orthography, which
was very peculiar, but translate it into legible English.
It ran thus:

"Your hellish machinery is shivered to smash on Stilbro' Moor, and your men are lying bound hand and foot in
a ditch by the roadside. Take this as a warning from men
that are starving and have starving wives and children
to go home to when they have done this deed. If you
get new machines, or if you otherwise go on as you have
done, you shall hear from us again. Beware!"

"Hear from you again? Yes; I'll hear from you again, and you shall hear from me. I'll speak to you directly; on Stilbro' Moor you shall hear from me in a moment."

Having led the waggons within the gates, he hastened towards the cottage. Opening the door, he spoke a few words quickly but quietly to two females who ran to meet him in the passage. He calmed the seeming alarm of one by a brief palliative account of what had taken place; to the other he said:

"Go into the mill, Sarah—there is the key—and ring the mill-bell as loud as you can; afterwards you will get another lantern, and help me to light up the front."

Returning to his horses, he unharnessed, fed, and stabled them with equal speed and care, pausing occasionally while so occupied, as if to listen for the mill-bell. It clanged out presently, with irregular but loud and alarming din; the hurried, agitated peal seemed more urgent than if the summons had been steadily given by a practised hand. On that still night, at that unusual hour, it was heard a long way round. The guests in the kitchen of the Redhouse were startled by the clangour; and, declaring that "there must be summat more nor common to do at Hollow's Miln," they called for lanterns, and hurried to the spot in a body. And scarcely had they thronged into the yard with their gleaming lights, when the tramp of horses was heard, and a little man in a shovel hat, sitting erect on the back of a shaggy pony, "rode lightly in," followed by an aide-de-camp mounted on a larger steed.

Mr Moore, meantime, after stabling his dray-horses, had saddled his hackney, and, with the aid of Sarah, the servant, lit up his mill, whose wide and long front now glared one great illumination, throwing a sufficient light on the yard to obviate all fear of confusion arising from obscurity. Already a deep hum of voices became audible. Mr Malone had at length issued from the counting-house, previously taking the precaution to dip

his head and face in the stone water-jar; and this precaution, together with the sudden alarm, had nearly
restored to him the possession of those senses which the
punch had partially scattered. He stood with his hat
on the back of his head and his shillelagh grasped in
his dexter fist, answering much at random the questions
of the newly-arrived party from the Redhouse. Mr
Moore now appeared, and was immediately confronted
by the shovel hat and the shaggy pony.

"Well, Moore, what is your business with us? I
thought you would want us to-night, me and the hetman
here" (patting his pony's neck), "and Tom and his
charger. When I heard your mill-bell, I could sit still no
longer, so I left Boultby to finish his supper alone; but
where is the enemy? I do not see a mask or a smutted
face present; and there is not a pane of glass broken in
your windows. Have you had an attack or do you expect
one?"

"Oh, not at all! I have neither had one nor expect
one," answered Moore coolly. "I only ordered the bell
to be rung because I want two or three neighbours to
stay here in the Hollow while I and a couple or so more
go over to Stilbro' Moor."

"To Stilbro' Moor! What to do? To meet the
waggons?"

"The waggons are come home an hour ago."

"Then all's right. What more would you have?"

"They came home empty, and Joe Scott and company
are left on the moor, and so are the frames. Read that
scrawl."

Mr Helstone received and perused the document of
which the contents have before been given.

"Hum! They've only served you as they serve others.
But, however, the poor fellows in the ditch will be
expecting help with some impatience: this is a wet night
for such a berth. I and Tom will go with you; Malone
may stay behind and take care of the mill: what is the

T   10

matter with him? His eyes seem starting out of his head."

"He has been eating a mutton-chop."

"Indeed! Peter Augustus, be on your guard. Eat no more mutton-chops to-night. You are left here in command of these premises—an honourable post."

"Is anybody to stay with me?"

"As many of the present assemblage as choose. My lads, how many of you will remain here, and how many will go a little way with me and Mr Moore on the Stilbro' road, to meet some men who have been waylaid and assaulted by frame-breakers?"

The small number of three volunteered to go, the rest preferred staying behind. As Mr Moore mounted his horse, the Rector asked him in a low voice whether he had locked up the mutton-chops, so that Peter Augustus could not get at them. The manufacturer nodded an affirmative, and the rescue party set out.

Cheerfulness, it would appear, is a matter which depends fully as much on the state of things within, as on the state of things without and around us. I make this trite remark, because I happen to know that Messrs Helstone and Moore trotted forth from the mill-yard gates, at the head of their very small company, in the best possible spirits. When a ray from a lantern (the three pedestrians of the party each carried one) fell on Mr Moore's face, you could see an unusual, because a lively, spark dancing in his eyes, and a new-found vivacity mantling on his dark physiognomy; and when the Rector's visage was illuminated, his hard features were revealed all agrin and ashine with glee. Yet a drizzling night, a somewhat perilous expedition, you would think were not circumstances calculated to enliven those exposed to the wet and engaged in the adventure. If any member or members of the crew who had been at work on Stilbro' Moor had caught a view of this party, they would have had great pleasure in shooting either of the leaders from behind a wall; and the leaders knew this; and, the fact is, being both men of steely nerves and steady-beating hearts, were elate with the knowledge.

I am aware, reader, and you need not remind me, that it is a dreadful thing for a parson to be warlike; I am aware that he should be a man of peace. I have some faint outline of an idea of what a clergyman's mission is amongst mankind, and I remember distinctly whose servant he is, whose message he delivers, whose example he should follow; yet, with all this, if you are a parson-hater, you need not expect me to go along with you every step of your dismal, downward-tending unchristian road; you need not expect me to join in your deep anathemas, at once so narrow and so sweeping—in your poisonous rancour, so intense and so absurd, against "the cloth"; to lift up my eyes and hands with a Supple-hough, or to inflate my lungs with a Barraclough, in horror and denunciation of the diabolical Rector of Briarfield.

He was not diabolical at all. The evil simply was, he had missed his vocation: he should have been a soldier, and circumstances had made him a priest. For the rest, he was a conscientious, hard-headed, hard-handed, brave, stern, implacable, faithful little man; a man almost without sympathy, ungentle, prejudiced, and rigid; but a man true to principle, honourable, sagacious, and sincere. It seems to me, reader, that you cannot always cut out men to fit their profession, and that you ought not to curse them because that profession some-times hangs on them ungracefully; nor will I curse Helstone, clerical Cossack as he was. Yet he *was* cursed, and by many of his own parishioners, as by others he was adored, which is the frequent fate of men who show partiality in friendship and bitterness in enmity; who are equally attached to principles and adherent to prejudices.

Helstone and Moore, being both in excellent spirits,

and united for the present in one cause, you would expect that, as they rode side by side, they would converse amicably. Oh no! These two men, of hard bilious natures both, rarely came into contact but they chafed each other's moods. Their frequent bone of contention was the war. Helstone was a high Tory (there were Tories in those days), and Moore was a bitter Whig— a Whig, at least, as far as opposition to the war-party was concerned, that being the question which affected his own interest; and only on that question did he profess any British politics at all. He liked to infuriate Helstone by declaring his belief in the invincibility of Bonaparte, by taunting England and Europe with the impotence of their efforts to withstand him, and by coolly advancing the opinion that it was as well to yield to him soon as late, since he must in the end crush every antagonist, and reign supreme.

Helstone could not bear these sentiments; it was only on the consideration of Moore being a sort of outcast and alien, and having but half-measure of British blood to temper the foreign gall which corroded his veins, that he brought himself to listen to them without indulging the wish he felt to cane the speaker. Another thing, too, somewhat allayed his disgust, namely, a fellow-feeling for the dogged tone with which these opinions were asserted, and a respect for the consistency of Moore's crabbed contumacy.

As the party turned into the Stilbro' road they met what little wind there was; the rain dashed in their faces. Moore had been fretting his companion previously, and now, braced up by the raw breeze, and perhaps irritated by the sharp drizzle, he began to goad him.

"Does your Peninsular news please you still?" he asked.

"What do you mean?" was the surly demand of the Rector.

"I mean have you still faith in that Baal of a Lord Wellington?"

"And what do you mean now?"

"Do you still believe that this wooden-faced and pebble-hearted idol of England has power to send fire down from heaven to consume the French holocaust you want to offer up?"

"I believe Wellington will flog Bonaparte's marshals into the sea the day it pleases him to lift his arm."

"But, my dear sir, you can't be serious in what you say. Bonaparte's marshals are great men, who act under the guidance of an omnipotent master-spirit; your Wellington is the most humdrum of commonplace martinets, whose slow mechanical movements are further cramped by an ignorant home Government."

"Wellington is the soul of England. Wellington is the right champion of a good cause; the fit representative of a powerful, a resolute, a sensible, and an honest nation."

"Your good cause, as far as I understand it, is simply the restoration of that filthy, feeble Ferdinand to a throne which he disgraced; your fit representative of an honest people is a dull-witted drover, acting for a duller-witted farmer; and against these are arrayed victorious supremacy and invincible genius."

"Against legitimacy is arrayed usurpation; against modest, single-minded, righteous, and brave resistance to encroachment, is arrayed boastful, double-tongued, selfish, and treacherous ambition to possess. God defend the right!"

"God often defends the powerful."

"What! I suppose the handful of Israelites standing dryshod on the Asiatic side of the Red Sea was more powerful than the host of the Egyptians drawn up on the African side? Were they more numerous? Were they better appointed? Were they more mighty, in a word—eh? Don't speak, or you'll tell a lie, Moore; you know you will. They were a poor overwrought band of bondsmen. Tyrants had oppressed them through four hundred years; a feeble mixture of women and children diluted their thin ranks; their masters, who roared to follow them through the divided flood, were a set of pampered Ethiops, about as strong and brutal as the lions of Libya. They were armed, horsed, and charioted; the poor Hebrew wanderers were afoot; few of them, it is likely, had better weapons than their shepherds' crooks, or their masons' building tools; their meek and mighty leader himself had only his rod. But bethink you, Robert Moore, right was with them; the God of battles was on their side. Crime and the lost archangel generalled the ranks of Pharaoh, and which triumphed? We know that well: 'The Lord saved Israel that day out of the hand of the Egyptians, and Israel saw the Egyptians dead upon the sea-shore'; yea, 'the depths covered them, they sank to the bottom as a stone.' The right hand of the Lord became glorious in power; the right hand of the Lord dashed in pieces the enemy!"

"You are all right, only you forget the true parallel. France is Israel, and Napoleon is Moses. Europe, with her old, overgorged empires and rotten dynasties, is corrupt Egypt: gallant France is the Twelve Tribes, and her fresh and vigorous Usurper the Shepherd of Horeb."

"I scorn to answer you."

Moore accordingly answered himself—at least, he subjoined to what he had just said an additional observation in a lower voice:

"Oh! in Italy he was as great as any Moses. He was the right thing there—fit to head and organize measures for the regeneration of nations. It puzzles me to this day how the conqueror of Lodi should have condescended to become an emperor—a vulgar, a stupid humbug!— and still more how a people who had once called themselves republicans should have sunk again to the grade of mere slaves. I despise France! If England had gone as far on the march of civilization as France did, she would hardly have retreated so shamelessly."

"You don't mean to say that besotted imperial France

is any worse than bloody republican France?" demanded
Helstone fiercely.

"I mean to say nothing: but I can think what I please,
you know, Mr Helstone, both about France and England;
and about revolutions, and regicides, and restorations
in general; and about the divine right of kings, which
you often stickle for in your sermons, and the duty of
non-resistance, and the sanity of war, and——"

Mr Moore's sentence was here cut short by the rapid
rolling up of a gig, and its sudden stoppage in the middle
of the road. Both he and the Rector had been too much
occupied with their discourse to notice its approach till
it was close upon them.

"Nah, maister, did th' waggons hit home?" demanded
a voice from the vehicle.

"Can that be Joe Scott?"

"Ay, ay!" returned another voice; for the gig contained two persons, as was seen by the glimmer of its
lamp. The men with the lanterns had now fallen into
the rear, or, rather, the equestrians of the rescue-party
had outridden the pedestrians. "Ay, Mr Moore, it's
Joe Scott. I'm bringing him back to you in a bonny
pickle. I fand him on the top of the moor yonder—him
and three others. What will you give me for restoring
him to you?"

"Why, my thanks, I believe: for I could better have
afforded to lose a better man. That is you, I suppose,
Mr Yorke, by your voice?"

"Ay, lad, it's me. I was coming home from Stilbro'
market, and just as I got to the middle of the moor, and
was whipping on as swift as the wind (for these, they say,
are not safe times, thanks to a bad Government!), I heard
a groan. I pulled up—some would have whipped on
faster, but I've naught to fear, that I know of. I don't
believe there's a lad in these parts would harm me—at
least, I'd give them as good as I got if they offered to do
it. I said, 'Is there aught wrong anywhere?' ''Deed is

there,' somebody says, speaking out of the ground, like.
'What's to do? Be sharp, and tell me!' I ordered.
'Nobbut four on us ligging in a ditch,' says Joe, as quiet
as could be. I tell'd 'em 'More shame to 'em,' and bid
them get up and move on, or I'd lend them a lick of the
gig-whip; for my notion was they were all fresh. 'We'd
ha done that an hour sin', but we're teed wi' a bit o'
band,' says Joe. So in a while I got down and loosed 'em
wi' my penknife, and Scott would ride wi' me to tell me
all how it happened, and t'others are coming on as fast
as their feet will bring them."

"Well, I am greatly obliged to you, Mr Yorke."

"Are you, my lad? You know you're not. However,
here are the rest approaching. And here, by the Lord!
is another set with lights in their pitchers, like the army
of Gideon, and as we've th' parson wi' us—good evening,
Mr Helstone—we'se do."

Mr Helstone returned the salutation of the individual
in the gig very stiffly indeed. That individual proceeded:

"We're eleven strong men, and there's both horses and
chariots amang us. If we could only fall in wi' some of
these starved ragamuffins of frame-breakers, we could
win a grand victory; we could iv'ry one be a Wellington
—that would please ye, Mr Helstone! And sich paragraphs as we could contrive for t' papers! Briarfield suld
be famous. But we'se hev a column and a half i' th'
Stilbro' Courier ower this job as it is, I dare say—I'se
expect no less."

"And I'll promise you no less, Mr Yorke, for I'll write
the article myself," returned the Rector.

"To be sure! sartainly! And mind ye recommend
weel that them 'at brake t' bits o' frames, and teed Joe
Scott's legs wi' band, suld be hung without benefit
o' clergy. It's a hanging matter, or suld be; no doubt
o' that."

"If I judged them, I'd give them short shrift!" cried
Moore; "but I mean to let them quite alone this bout,

to give them rope enough, certain that in the end they will hang themselves."

"Let them alone, will ye, Moore? Do you promise that?"

"Promise! No. All I mean to say is, I shall give myself no particular trouble to catch them; but if one falls in my way——"

"You'll snap him up, of course; only you would rather they would do something worse than merely stop a waggon before you reckon with them. Well, we'll say no more on the subject at present. Here we are at my door, gentlemen, and I hope you and the men will step in; you will none of you be the worse of a little refreshment."

THE CURATES AT TEA

from Shirley.

SUDDENLY the door-bell sharply rang. Her heart leaped. She sprang to the drawing-room door, opened it softly, peeped through the aperture. Fanny was admitting a visitor, a gentleman—a tall man, just the height of Robert. For one second she thought it was Robert, for one second she exulted; but the voice asking for Mr Helstone undeceived her: that voice was an Irish voice, consequently not Moore's, but the curate's, Malone's. He was ushered into the dining-room, where, doubtless, he speedily helped his Rector to empty the decanters.

It was a fact to be noted that, at whatever house in Briarfield, Whinbury or Nunnely, one curate dropped in to a meal—dinner or tea, as the case might be—another presently followed, often two more. Not that they gave each other the rendezvous, but they were usually all on the run at the same time, and when Donne, for instance, sought Malone at his lodgings and found him not, he inquired whither he had posted, and, having learned of the landlady his destination, hastened with all speed after him. The same causes operated in the same way with Sweeting. Thus it chanced on that afternoon that Caroline's ears were three times tortured with the ringing of the bell, and the advent of undesired guests— for Donne followed Malone, and Sweeting followed Donne, and more wine was ordered up from the cellar into the dining-room (for, though old Helstone chid the inferior priesthood when he found them "carousing," as he called it, in their own tents, yet at his hierarchical table he ever liked to treat them to a glass of his best), and through the closed doors Caroline heard their boyish laughter and the vacant cackle of their voices. Her fear was lest they should stay to tea, for she had no pleasure in making tea for that particular trio. What distinctions people draw! These three were men, young men, educated men, like Moore: yet, for her, how great the difference! Their society was a bore, his a delight.

Not only was she destined to be favoured with their clerical company, but Fortune was at this moment bringing her four other guests—lady guests, all packed in a pony-phaeton now rolling somewhat heavily along the road from Whinbury. An elderly lady and three of her buxom daughters were coming to see her "in a friendly way," as the custom of that neighbourhood was. Yes, a fourth time the bell clanged. Fanny brought the present announcement to the drawing-room:

"Mrs Sykes and the three Misses Sykes."

When Caroline was going to receive company, her habit was to wring her hands very nervously, to flush a little, and come forward hurriedly yet hesitatingly, wishing herself meantime at Jericho. She was, at such crises, sadly deficient in finished manner, though she had once been at school a year. Accordingly, on this occasion, her small white hands sadly maltreated each other while she stood up waiting the entrance of Mrs Sykes.

In stalked that lady, a tall, bilious gentlewoman, who made an ample and not altogether insincere profession of piety, and was greatly given to hospitality towards the clergy. In sailed her three daughters, a showy trio, being all three well-grown and more or less handsome.

In English country ladies there is this point to be remarked. Whether young or old, pretty or plain, dull or sprightly, they all (or most all) have a certain expression stamped on their features, which seems to say, "I know —I do not boast of it—but I *know* that I am the standard of what is proper. Let everyone, therefore, whom I approach, or who approaches me, keep a sharp look-out, for wherein they differ from me—be the same in dress, manner, opinion, principle, or practice—therein they are wrong."

Mrs and Misses Sykes, far from being exceptions to this observation, were pointed illustrations of its truth. Miss Mary—a well-looked, well-meant, and, on the whole, well-dispositioned girl—wore her complacency with some state, though without harshness; Miss Harriet —a beauty—carried it more overbearingly; she looked high and cold; Miss Hannah, who was conceited, dashing, pushing, flourished hers consciously and openly; the mother evinced it with the gravity proper to her age and religious fame.

The reception was got through somehow. Caroline "was glad to see them" (an unmitigated fib), hoped they were well, hoped Mrs Sykes's cough was better (Mrs Sykes had had a cough for the last twenty years), hoped the Misses Sykes had left their sisters at home well; to which inquiry the Misses Sykes, sitting on three chairs opposite the music stool whereon Caroline had undesignedly come to anchor, after wavering for some seconds between it and a large arm-chair, into which she at length recollected she ought to induct Mrs Sykes, and, indeed, that lady saved her the trouble by depositing herself therein; the Misses Sykes replied to Caroline by one simultaneous bow, very majestic and mighty awful. A pause followed; this bow was of a character to insure silence for the next five minutes, and it did. Mrs Sykes then inquired after Mr Helstone, and whether he had had any return of rheumatism, and whether preaching twice on a Sunday fatigued him, and if he was capable of taking a full service now, and, on being assured he was, she and all her daughters, combining in chorus, expressed their opinion that he was "a wonderful man of his years."

Pause second.

Miss Mary, getting up the steam in her turn, asked whether Caroline had attended the Bible Society meeting which had been held at Nunnely last Thursday night; the negative answer which truth compelled Caroline to utter—for last Thursday evening she had been sitting at home reading a novel which Robert had lent her—elicited a simultaneous expression of surprise from the lips of the four ladies.

"We were all there," said Miss Mary; "mamma and all of us; we even persuaded papa to go; Hannah would insist upon it; but he fell asleep while Mr Langweilig, the German Moravian minister, was speaking; I felt quite ashamed, he nodded so."

"And there was Dr Broadbent," cried Hannah, "such a beautiful speaker! You couldn't expect it of him, for he is almost a vulgar-looking man."

"But such a dear man!" interrupted Mary.

"And such a good man, such a useful man," added her mother.

"Only like a butcher in appearance," interposed the fair, proud Harriet. "I couldn't bear to look at him; I listened with my eyes shut."

Miss Helstone felt her ignorance and incompetency; not having seen Dr Broadbent, she could not give her opinion. Pause third came on. During its continuance

Caroline was feeling at her heart's core what a dreaming fool she was, what an unpractical life she led, how little fitness there was in her for ordinary intercourse with the ordinary world. She was feeling how exclusively she had attached herself to the white cottage in the Hollow, how in the existence of one inmate of that cottage she had pent all her universe; she was sensible that this would not do, and that some day she would be forced to make an alteration; it could not be said that she exactly wished to resemble the ladies before her, but she wished to become superior to her present self, so as to feel less scared by their dignity.

The sole means she found of reviving the flagging discourse was by asking them if they would all stay to tea; and a cruel struggle it cost her to perform this piece of civility. Mrs Sykes had begun, "We are much obliged to you, but——" when in came Fanny once more.

"The gentlemen will stay the evening, ma'am," was the message she brought from Mr Helstone.

"What gentlemen have you?" now inquired Mrs Sykes.

Their names were specified; she and her daughters interchanged glances; the curates were not to them what they were to Caroline. Mr Sweeting was quite a favourite with them; even Mr Malone rather so, because he was a clergyman.

"Really, since you have company already, I think we will stay," remarked Mrs Sykes. "We shall be quite a pleasant little party; I always like to meet the clergy."

And now Caroline had to usher them upstairs, to help them to unshawl, smooth their hair, and make themselves smart; to reconduct them to the drawing-room, to distribute amongst them books of engravings, or odd things purchased from the Jew-basket; she was obliged to be a purchaser, though she was but a slack contributor; and if she had possessed plenty of money, she would rather, when it was brought to the Rectory—an awful incubus!—have purchased the whole stock, than contributed a single pincushion.

It ought perhaps to be explained in passing, for the benefit of those who are not "au fait" to the mysteries of the "Jew-basket" and "Missionary-basket," that these "meubles" are willow-repositories, of the capacity of a good-sized family clothes-basket, dedicated to the purpose of conveying from house to house a monster collection of pincushions, needle-books, card-racks, work-bags, articles of infant wear, etc., made by the willing or reluctant hands of the Christian ladies of a parish, and sold perforce to the heathenish gentlemen thereof at prices unblushingly exorbitant. The proceeds of such compulsory sales are applied to the conversion of the Jews, the seeking up of the ten missing tribes, or to the regeneration of the interesting coloured population of the globe. Each lady contributor takes it in her turn to keep the basket a month, to sew for it, and to foist off its contents on a shrinking male public. An exciting time it is when that turn comes round: some active-minded women, with a good trading spirit, like it, and enjoy exceedingly the fun of making hard-handed worsted-spinners cash up, to the tune of four or five hundred per cent. above cost price, for articles quite useless to them; other feebler souls object to it, and would rather see the prince of darkness himself at their door any morning than that phantom-basket, brought with "Mrs Rouse's compliments, and please, ma'am, she says it's your turn now."

Miss Helstone's duties of hostess performed, more anxiously than cheerily, she betook herself to the kitchen, to hold a brief privy-council with Fanny and Eliza about the tea.

"What a lot on 'em!" cried Eliza, who was cook. "And I put off the baking to-day because I thought there would be bread plenty to fit while morning: we shall never have enow."

"Are there any tea-cakes?" asked the young mistress.

"Only three and a loaf. I wish these fine folk would stay at home till they're asked; and I want to finish trimming my hat" (bonnet she meant).

"Then," suggested Caroline, to whom the importance of the emergency gave a certain energy, "Fanny must run down to Briarfield and buy some muffins and crumpets, and some biscuits; and don't be cross, Eliza, we can't help it now."

"And which tea-things are we to have?"

"Oh, the best, I suppose! I'll get out the silver service," and she ran upstairs to the plate-closet, and presently brought down teapot, cream-ewer, and sugar-basin.

"And mun we have th' urn?"

"Yes; and now get it ready as quickly as you can, for the sooner we have tea over, the sooner they will go— at least, I hope so. Heigho! I wish they were gone," she sighed, as she returned to the drawing-room. "Still," she thought, as she paused at the door ere opening it, "if Robert would but come even now, how bright all would be! How comparatively easy the task of amusing these people, if he were present! There would be an interest in hearing him talk (though he never says much in company), and in talking in his presence: there can be no interest in hearing any of them, or in speaking to them. How they will gabble when the curates come in, and how weary I shall grow with listening to them! But I suppose I am a selfish fool! These are very respectable gentlefolks; I ought, no doubt, to be proud of their countenance. I don't say they are not as good as I am —far from it—but they are different from me."

She went in.

Yorkshire people, in those days, took their tea round the table, sitting well into it, with their knees duly introduced under the mahogany. It was essential to have a multitude of plates of bread-and-butter, varied in sorts and plentiful in quantity; it was thought proper, too, that on the centre-plate should stand a glass dish of marmalade; among the viands was expected to be found a small assortment of cheesecakes and tarts; if there was also a plate of thin slices of pink ham garnished with green parsley, so much the better.

Eliza, the Rector's cook, fortunately knew her business as provider. She had been put out of humour a little at first, when the invaders came so unexpectedly in such strength; but it appeared that she regained her cheerfulness with action, for in due time the tea was spread forth in handsome style, and neither ham, tarts, nor marmalade were wanting among its accompaniments.

The curates, summoned to this bounteous repast, entered joyous; but at once, on seeing the ladies, of whose presence they had not been forewarned, they came to a stand in the doorway. Malone headed the party; he stopped short and fell back, almost capsizing Donne, who was behind him. Donne, staggering three paces in retreat, sent little Sweeting into the arms of old Helstone, who brought up the rear. There was some expostulation, some tittering: Malone was desired to mind what he was about, and urged to push forward, which at last he did, though colouring to the top of his peaked forehead a bluish purple. Helstone, advancing, set the shy curates aside, welcomed all his fair guests, shook hands and passed a jest with each, and seated himself snugly between the lovely Harriet and the dashing Hannah; Miss Mary he requested to move to the seat opposite to him, that he might see her if he couldn't be near her. Perfectly easy and gallant, in his way, were his manners always to young ladies; and most popular was he amongst them: yet, at heart, he neither respected nor liked the sex, and such of them as circumstances had brought into intimate relation with him had ever feared rather than loved him.

The curates were left to shift for themselves. Sweeting, who was the least embarrassed of the three, took refuge

beside Mrs Sykes; who, he knew, was almost as fond of
him as if he had been her son. Donne, after making his
general bow, with a grace all his own, and saying in a
high pragmatical voice, "How d'ye do, Miss Helstone?"
dropped into a seat at Caroline's elbow, to her unmitigated annoyance, for she had a peculiar antipathy to
Donne, on account of his stultified and unmovable self-
conceit, and his incurable narrowness of mind. Malone,
grinning most unmeaningly, inducted himself into the
corresponding seat on the other side: she was thus blessed
in a pair of supporters, neither of whom, she knew, would
be of any mortal use, whether for keeping up the conversation, handing cups, circulating the muffins, or even
lifting the plate from the slop-basin. Little Sweeting,
small and boyish as he was, would have been worth
twenty of them.

Malone, though a ceaseless talker when there were
only men present, was usually tongue-tied in the presence
of ladies: three phrases, however, he had ready cut and
dried, which he never failed to produce:

Firstly: "Have you had a walk to-day, Miss Helstone?"

Secondly: "Have you seen your cousin, Moore, lately?"

Thirdly: "Does your class at the Sunday-school keep
up its number?"

These three questions being put and responded to,
between Caroline and Malone reigned silence.

With Donne it was otherwise: he was troublesome,
exasperating. He had a stock of small-talk on hand,
at once the most trite and perverse that can well be
imagined: abuse of the people of Briarfield; of the natives
of Yorkshire generally; complaints of the want of high
society, of the backward state of civilization in these
districts; murmurings against the disrespectful conduct
of the lower orders in the north toward their betters;
silly ridicule of the manner of living in these parts—the
want of style, the absence of elegance, as if he, Donne,
had been accustomed to very great doings indeed: an

insinuation which his somewhat underbred manner and aspect failed to bear out. These strictures, he seemed to think, must raise him in the estimation of Miss Helstone, or of any other lady who heard him; whereas with her, at least, they brought him to a level below contempt; though sometimes, indeed, they incensed her; for, a Yorkshire girl herself, she hated to hear Yorkshire abused by such a pitiful prater; and when brought up to a certain pitch, she would turn and say something of which neither the matter nor the manner recommended her to Mr Donne's good-will. She would tell him it was no proof of refinement to be ever scolding others for vulgarity; and no sign of a good pastor to be eternally censuring his flock. She would ask him what he had entered the Church for, since he complained there were only cottages to visit and poor people to preach to—whether he had been ordained to the ministry merely to wear soft clothing and sit in kings' houses? These questions were considered by all the curates as, to the last degree, audacious and impious.

Tea was a long time in progress; all the guests gabbled as their hostess had expected they would. Mr Helstone, being in excellent spirits—when, indeed, was he ever otherwise in society, attractive female society?—it being only with the one lady of his own family that he maintained a grim taciturnity, kept up a brilliant flow of easy prattle with his right-hand and left-hand neighbours, and even with his *vis-à-vis*, Miss Mary: though as Mary was the most sensible, the least coquettish of the three, to her the elderly widower was the least attentive. At heart, he could not abide sense in women: he liked to see them as silly, as light-headed, as vain, as open to ridicule as possible: because they were then in reality what he held them to be, and wished them to be—inferior: toys to play with, to amuse a vacant hour and to be thrown away.

Hannah was his favourite. Harriet, though beautiful,

egotistical, and self-satisfied, was not quite weak enough for him: she had some genuine self-respect amidst much false pride, and if she did not talk like an oracle, neither would she babble like one crazy: she would not permit herself to be treated quite as a doll, a child, a plaything: she expected to be bent to like a queen.

Hannah, on the contrary, demanded no respect; only flattery: if her admirers only *told* her that she was an angel, she would let them *treat* her like an idiot. So very credulous and frivolous was she, so very silly did she become when besieged with attention, flattered and admired to the proper degree, that there were moments when Helstone actually felt tempted to commit matrimony a second time, and to try the experiment of taking her for his second helpmeet; but, fortunately, the salutary recollection of the ennuis of his first marriage, the impression still left on him of the weight of the millstone he had once worn round his neck, the fixity of his feelings respecting the insufferable evils of conjugal existence, operated as a check to his tenderness, suppressed the sigh heaving his old iron lungs, and restrained him from whispering to Hannah proposals it would have been high fun and great satisfaction to her to hear.

It is probable she would have married him if he had asked her; her parents would have quite approved the match. To them his fifty-five years, his bend-leather heart, could have presented no obstacles; and as he was a Rector, held an excellent living, occupied a good house, and was supposed even to have private property (though in that the world was mistaken; every penny of the £5000 inherited by him from his father had been devoted to the building and endowing of a new church at his native village in Lancashire—for he could show a lordly munificence when he pleased, and, if the end was to his liking, never hesitated about making a grand sacrifice to attain it)—her parents, I say, would have delivered Hannah over to his lovingkindness and his tender mercies without one scruple; and the second Mrs Helstone, inverting the natural order of insect existence, would have fluttered through the honeymoon a bright, admired butterfly, and crawled the rest of her days a sordid trampled worm.

Little Mr Sweeting, seated between Mrs Sykes and Miss Mary, both of whom were very kind to him, and having a dish of tarts before him, and marmalade and crumpet upon his plate, looked and felt more content than any monarch. He was fond of all the Misses Sykes; they were all fond of him. He thought them magnificent girls, quite proper to mate with one of his inches. If he had a cause of regret at this blissful moment, it was that Miss Dora happened to be absent, Dora being the one whom he secretly hoped one day to call Mrs David Sweeting, with whom he dreamt of taking stately walks, leading her like an Empress through the village of Nunnely. And an Empress she would have been, if size could make an Empress. She was vast, ponderous; seen from behind, she had the air of a very stout lady of forty, but withal she possessed a good face, and no unkindly character.

The meal at last drew to a close; it would have been over long ago if Mr Donne had not persisted in sitting with his cup half-full of cold tea before him, long after the rest had finished, and after he himself had discussed such allowance of viands as he felt competent to swallow —long, indeed, after signs of impatience had been manifested all round the board, till chairs were pushed back, till the talk flagged, till silence fell. Vainly did Caroline inquire repeatedly if he would have another cup, if he would take a little hot tea, as that must be cold, etc.; he would neither drink it nor leave it. He seemed to think that this isolated position of his gave him somehow a certain importance; that it was dignified and stately to be the last; that it was grand to keep all the others waiting. So long did he linger that the very urn died;

it ceased to hiss. At length, however, the old Rector himself, who had hitherto been too pleasantly engaged with Hannah to care for the delay, got impatient.

"For whom are we waiting?" he asked.

"For me, I believe," returned Donne complacently, appearing to think it much to his credit that a party should thus be kept dependent on his movements.

"Tut!" cried Helstone. Then, standing up, "Let us return thanks," said he, which he did forthwith, and all quitted the table.

Donne, nothing abashed, still sat ten minutes quite alone, whereupon Mr Helstone rang the bell for the things to be removed. The curate at length saw himself forced to empty his cup, and to relinquish the rôle which he thought had given him such a felicitous distinction, drawn upon him such flattering general notice.

And now, in the natural course of events (Caroline, knowing how it would be, had opened the piano, and produced music-books in readiness), music was asked for. This was Mr Sweeting's chance for showing off; he was eager to commence. He undertook, therefore, the arduous task of persuading the young ladies to favour the company with an air—a song. *Con amore*, he went through the whole business of begging, praying, resisting excuses, explaining away difficulties, and at last succeeded in persuading Miss Harriet to allow herself to be led to the instrument. Then out came the pieces of his flute (he always carried them in his pocket, as unfailingly as he carried his handkerchief). They were screwed and arranged, Malone and Donne meantime herding together and sneering at him, which the little man, glancing over his shoulder, saw, but did not heed at all; he was persuaded their sarcasm all arose from envy. They could not accompany the ladies as he could; he was about to enjoy a triumph over them.

The triumph began. Malone, much chagrined at hearing him pipe up in most superior style, determined to earn distinction, too, if possible, and all at once assuming the character of a swain (which character he had endeavoured to enact once or twice before, but in which he had not hitherto met with the success he doubtless opined his merits deserved), approached a sofa on which Miss Helstone was seated, and depositing his great Irish frame near her, tried his hand (or, rather, tongue) at a fine speech or two, accompanied by grins the most extraordinary and incomprehensible. In the course of his efforts to render himself agreeable, he contrived to possess himself of the two long sofa cushions and a square one; with which, after rolling them about for some time with strange gestures, he managed to erect a sort of barrier between himself and the object of his attentions. Caroline, quite willing that they should be sundered, soon devised an excuse for stepping over to the opposite side of the room, and taking up a position beside Mrs Sykes, of which good lady she entreated some instruction in a new stitch in ornamental knitting, a favour readily granted, and thus Peter Augustus was thrown out.

Very sullenly did his countenance lower when he saw himself abandoned—left entirely to his own resources, on a large sofa, with the charge of three small cushions on his hands. The fact was, he felt disposed seriously to cultivate acquaintance with Miss Helstone; because he thought, in common with others, that her uncle possessed money, and concluded that since he had no children he would probably leave it to his niece. Gérard Moore was better instructed on this point; he had seen the neat church that owed its origin to the Rector's zeal and cash, and more than once, in his inmost soul, had cursed an expensive caprice which crossed his wishes.

The evening seemed long to one person in that room. Caroline at intervals dropped her knitting on her lap, and gave herself up to a sort of brain-lethargy—closing her eyes and depressing her head—caused by what seemed to her the unmeaning hum around her; the inharmonious, tasteless rattle of the piano-keys, the squeaking and gasping notes of the flute, the laughter and mirth of her uncle and Hannah and Mary, she could not tell whence originating, for she heard nothing comic or gleeful in their discourse; and, more than all, by the interminable gossip of Mrs Sykes, murmured close at her ear, gossip which rang the changes on four subjects —her own health and that of the various members of her family, the missionary and Jew baskets and their contents, the late meeting at Nunnely, and one which was expected to come off next week at Whinbury.

Tired at length to exhaustion, she embraced the opportunity of Mr Sweeting coming up to speak to Mrs Sykes to slip quietly out of the apartment and seek a moment's respite in solitude. She repaired to the dining-room, where the clear but now low remnant of a fire still burnt in the grate. The place was empty and quiet, glasses and decanters were cleared from the table, the chairs were put back in their places, all was orderly. Caroline sank into her uncle's large easy-chair, half shut her eyes, and rested herself—rested at least her limbs, her senses, her hearing, her vision—weary with listening to nothing and gazing on vacancy....

Here the company was heard rising in the other room; the door was opened, the pony-carriage was ordered, shawls and bonnets were demanded. Mr Helstone called for his niece.

THE FOUNDLING

from *Wuthering Heights*.

BEFORE I came to live here, she commenced—waiting no farther invitation to her story—I was almost always at Wuthering Heights; because my mother had nursed Mr Hindley Earnshaw, that was Hareton's father, and I got used to playing with the children: I ran errands too, and helped to make hay, and hung about the farm ready for anything that anybody would set me to. One fine summer morning—it was the beginning of harvest, I remember—Mr Earnshaw, the old master, came downstairs, dressed for a journey; and after he had told Joseph what was to be done during the day, he turned to Hindley, and Cathy, and me—for I sat eating my porridge with them—and he said, speaking to his son, "Now, my bonny man, I'm going to Liverpool to-day, what shall I bring you? You may choose what you like: only let it be little, for I shall walk there and back: sixty miles each way, that is a long spell!" Hindley named a fiddle, and then he asked Miss Cathy; she was hardly six years old, but she could ride any horse in the stable, and she chose a whip. He did not forget me; for he had a kind heart, though he was rather severe sometimes. He promised to bring me a pocketful of apples and pears, and then he kissed his children, said good-bye, and set off.

It seemed a long while to us all—the three days of his absence—and often did little Cathy ask when he would be home. Mrs Earnshaw expected him by supper-time, on the third evening, and she put the meal off hour after hour; there were no signs of his coming, however, and at last the children got tired of running down to the gate to look. Then it grew dark; she would have had them to bed, but they begged sadly to be allowed to stay up; and, just about eleven o'clock, the door-latch was raised quietly, and in stepped the master. He threw himself into a chair, laughing and groaning, and bid them all stand off, for he was nearly killed—he would not have such another walk for the three kingdoms.

"And at the end of it, to be flighted to death!" he said, opening his great-coat, which he held bundled up in his arms. "See here, wife! I was never so beaten with anything in my life: but you must e'en take it as a gift of God; though it's as dark almost as if it came from the devil."

We crowded round, and over Miss Cathy's head I had a peep at a dirty, ragged, black-haired child; big enough both to walk and talk: indeed, its face looked older than Catherine's; yet, when it was set on its feet, it only stared round, and repeated over and over again some gibberish that nobody could understand. I was frightened, and Mrs Earnshaw was ready to fling it out of doors: she did fly up, asking how he could fashion to bring that gipsy brat into the house, when they had their own bairns to feed and fend for? What he meant to do with it, and whether he were mad? The master tried to explain the matter; but he was really half dead with fatigue, and all that I could make out, amongst her scolding, was a tale of his seeing it starving, and houseless, and as good as dumb, in the streets of Liverpool; where he picked it up and inquired for its owner. Not a soul knew to whom it belonged, he said; and his money and time being both limited, he thought it better to take it home with him at once, than run into vain expenses there: because he was determined he would not leave it as he found it. Well, the conclusion was that my mistress grumbled herself calm; and Mr Earnshaw told me to wash it, and give it clean things, and let it sleep with the children.

Hindley and Cathy contented themselves with looking and listening till peace was restored: then, both began searching their father's pockets for the presents he had promised them. The former was a boy of fourteen, but when he drew out what had been a fiddle, crushed to morsels in the great-coat, he blubbered aloud; and Cathy, when she learned the master had lost her whip in attending on the stranger, showed her humour by grinning and spitting at the stupid little thing; earning for her pains a sound blow from her father to teach her cleaner manners. They entirely refused to have it in bed with them, or even in their room; and I had no more sense, so I put it on the landing of the stairs, hoping it might be gone on the morrow. By chance, or else attracted by hearing his voice, it crept to Mr Earnshaw's door, and there he found it on quitting his chamber. Inquiries were made as to how it got there; I was obliged to confess, and in recompense for my cowardice and inhumanity was sent out of the house.

This was Heathcliff's first introduction to the family. On coming back a few days afterwards (for I did not consider my banishment perpetual) I found they had christened him "Heathcliff": it was the name of a son who died in childhood, and it has served him ever since, both for Christian and surname. Miss Cathy and he were now very thick; but Hindley hated him: and to say the truth I did the same; and we plagued and went on with him shamefully: for I wasn't reasonable enough to feel my injustice, and the mistress never put in a word on his behalf when she saw him wronged.

He seemed a sullen, patient child; hardened, perhaps, to ill-treatment: he would stand Hindley's blows without winking or shedding a tear, and my pinches moved him only to draw in a breath and open his eyes, as if he had hurt himself by accident and nobody was to blame. This endurance made old Earnshaw furious, when he discovered his son persecuting the poor, fatherless child, as he called him. He took to Heathcliff strangely, believing all he said (for that matter, he said precious little, and generally the truth), and petting him up far above Cathy, who was too mischievous and wayward for a favourite.

So, from the very beginning, he bred bad feeling in the house; and at Mrs Earnshaw's death, which happened in less than two years after, the young master had learned to regard his father as an oppressor rather than a friend, and Heathcliff as a usurper of his parent's affections and his privileges; and he grew bitter with brooding over these injuries. I sympathized a while; but when the children fell ill of the measles, and I had to tend them, and take on me the cares of a woman at once, I changed my ideas. Heathcliff was dangerously sick; and while he lay at the worst he would have me constantly by his pillow: I suppose he felt I did a good deal for him, and he hadn't wit to guess that I was compelled to do it. However, I will say this, he was the quietest child that ever nurse watched over. The difference between him and the others forced me to be less partial. Cathy and her brother harassed me terribly; *he* was as uncomplaining as a lamb; though hardness, not gentleness, made him give little trouble.

He got through, and the doctor affirmed it was in a great measure owing to me, and praised me for my care. I was vain of his commendations, and softened towards the being by whose means I earned them, and thus Hindley lost his last ally: still I couldn't dote on Heathcliff, and I wondered often what my master saw to admire so much in the sullen boy, who never, to my recollection, repaid his indulgence by any sign of gratitude. He was not insolent to his benefactor, he was simply insensible; though knowing perfectly the hold he had on his heart, and conscious he had only to speak and all the house would be obliged to bend to his wishes. As an instance, I remember Mr Earnshaw once bought a couple of colts at the parish fair, and gave the lads each one. Heathcliff took the handsomest, but it soon fell lame, and when he discovered it, he said to Hindley—

"You must exchange horses with me: I don't like mine; and if you won't I shall tell your father of the three thrashings you've given me this week, and show him my arm, which is black to the shoulder." Hindley put out his tongue, and cuffed him over the ears. "You'd better do it at once," he persisted, escaping to the porch (they were in the stable): "you will have to; and if I speak of these blows, you'll get them again with interest." "Off, dog!" cried Hindley, threatening him with an iron weight used for weighing potatoes and hay. "Throw it," he replied, standing still, "and then I'll tell how you boasted that you would turn me out of doors as soon as he died, and see whether he will not turn you out directly.'' Hindley threw it, hitting him on the breast, and down he fell, but staggered up immediately, breathless and white; and, had not I prevented it, he would have gone just so to the master, and got full revenge by letting his condition plead for him, intimating who had caused it. ''Take my colt, gipsy, then!'' said young Earnshaw. ''And I pray that he may break your neck: take him, and be damned, you beggarly interloper! and wheedle my father out of all he has: only afterwards show him what you are, imp of Satan.—And take that, I hope he'll kick out your brains!''

Heathcliff had gone to loose the beast, and shift it to his own stall; he was passing behind it, when Hindley finished his speech by knocking him under its feet, and without stopping to examine whether his hopes were fulfilled, ran away as fast as he could. I was surprised to witness how coolly the child gathered himself up, and went on with his intention; exchanging saddles and all, and then sitting down on a bundle of hay to overcome the qualm which the violent blow occasioned, before he entered the house. I persuaded him easily to let me lay the blame of his bruises on the horse: he minded little what tale was told since he had what he wanted. He complained so seldom, indeed, of such stirs as these, that I really thought him not vindictive: I was deceived completely, as you will hear.

In the course of time, Mr Earnshaw began to fail. He had been active and healthy, yet his strength left him suddenly; and when he was confined to the chimney-corner he grew grievously irritable. A nothing vexed him; and suspected slights of his authority nearly threw him into fits. This was especially to be remarked if any one attempted to impose upon, or domineer over, his favourite: he was painfully jealous lest a word should be spoken amiss to him; seeming to have got into his head the notion that, because he liked Heathcliff, all hated, and longed to do him an ill-turn. It was a disadvantage to the lad; for the kinder among us did not wish to fret the master, so we humoured his partiality; and that humouring was rich nourishment to the child's pride and black tempers. Still it became in a manner necessary; twice, or thrice, Hindley's manifestation of scorn, while his father was near, roused the old man to a fury: he seized his stick to strike him, and shook with rage that he could not do it.

At last, our curate (we had a curate then who made the living answer by teaching the little Lintons and Earnshaws, and farming his bit of land himself) advised that the young man should be sent to college; and Mr Earnshaw agreed, though with a heavy spirit, for he said—"Hindley was nought, and would never thrive as where he wandered."

I hoped heartily we should have peace now. It hurt me to think the master should be made uncomfortable by his own good deed. I fancied the discontent of age and disease arose from his family disagreements; as he would have it that it did: really, you know, sir, it was in his sinking frame. We might have got on tolerably, notwithstanding, but for two people, Miss Cathy and Joseph, the servant: you saw him, I dare say, up yonder. He was, and is yet most likely, the wearisomest, self-righteous pharisee that ever ransacked a Bible to rake the promises to himself and fling the curses to his neighbours. By his knack of sermonizing and pious discoursing, he contrived to make a great impression on Mr Earnshaw; and the more feeble the master became, the more influence he gained. He was relentless in worrying him about his soul's concerns, and about ruling his children rigidly. He encouraged him to regard Hindley as a reprobate; and, night after night, he regularly grumbled out a long string of tales against Heathcliff and Catherine: always minding to flatter Earnshaw's weakness by heaping the heaviest blame on the latter.

Certainly, she had ways with her such as I never saw a child take up before; and she put all of us past our patience fifty times and oftener in a day: from the hour she came down-stairs till the hour she went to bed, we had not a minute's security that she wouldn't be in mischief. Her spirits were always at high-water mark, her tongue always going—singing, laughing, and plaguing everybody who would not do the same. A wild, wicked slip she was—but she had the bonniest eye, the sweetest smile, and lightest foot in the parish: and, after all, I believe she meant no harm; for when once she made you cry in good earnest, it seldom happened that she would not keep you company, and oblige you to be quiet that you might comfort her. She was much too fond of Heathcliff. The greatest punishment we could invent for her was to keep her separate from him; yet she got chided more than any of us on his account. In play, she liked exceedingly to act the little mistress; using her hands freely, and commanding her companions: she did so to me, but I would not bear slapping and ordering; and so I let her know.

Now, Mr Earnshaw did not understand jokes from his children: he had always been strict and grave with them; and Catherine, on her part, had no idea why her father should be crosser and less patient in his ailing condition than he was in his prime. His peevish reproofs wakened in her a naughty delight to provoke him: she was never so happy as when we were all scolding her at once, and she defying us with her bold, saucy look, and her ready words; turning Joseph's religious curses into ridicule, baiting me, and doing just what her father hated most—showing how her pretended insolence, which he thought real, had more power over Heathcliff than his kindness: how the boy would do *her* bidding in anything, and *his* only when it suited his own inclination.

After behaving as badly as possible all day, she sometimes came fondling to make it up at night. "Nay,
Cathy," the old man would say, "I cannot love thee;
thou'rt worse than thy brother. Go, say thy prayers,
child, and ask God's pardon. I doubt thy mother and
I must rue that we ever reared thee!" That made her
cry, at first; and then being repulsed continually hardened
her, and she laughed if I told her to say she was sorry for
her faults, and beg to be forgiven.

But the hour came, at last, that ended Mr Earnshaw's
troubles on earth. He died quietly in his chair one
October evening, seated by the fire-side. A high wind
blustered round the house, and roared in the chimney:
it sounded wild and stormy, yet it was not cold, and we
were all together—I, a little removed from the hearth,
busy at my knitting, and Joseph reading his Bible near
the table (for the servants generally sat in the house then,
after their work was done). Miss Cathy had been sick,
and that made her still; she leant against her father's
knee, and Heathcliff was lying on the floor with his head
in her lap. I remember the master, before he fell into
a doze, stroking her bonny hair—it pleased him rarely
to see her gentle—and saying: "Why canst thou not
always be a good lass, Cathy?" And she turned her face
up to his, and laughed, and answered, "Why cannot you
always be a good man, father?" But as soon as she saw
him vexed again, she kissed his hand, and said she would
sing him to sleep. She began singing very low, till his
fingers dropped from hers, and his head sank on his
breast. Then I told her to hush, and not stir, for fear she
should wake him. We all kept as mute as mice a full
half-hour, and should have done so longer, only Joseph,
having finished his chapter, got up and said that he must
rouse the master for prayers and bed. He stepped forward,
and called him by name, and touched his shoulder; but
he would not move, so he took the candle and looked at
him. I thought there was something wrong as he set

down the light; and seizing the children each by an arm, whispered them to "frame up-stairs, and make little din —they might pray alone that evening—he had summut to do."

"I shall bid father good-night first," said Catherine, putting her arms round his neck, before we could hinder her. The poor thing discovered her loss directly—she screamed out—"Oh, he's dead, Heathcliff! he's dead!" And they both set up a heart-breaking cry.

I joined my wail to theirs, loud and bitter; but Joseph asked what we could be thinking of to roar in that way over a saint in heaven. He told me to put on my cloak and run to Gimmerton for the doctor and the parson. I could not guess the use that either would be of, then. However, I went, through wind and rain, and brought one, the doctor, back with me; the other said he would come in the morning. Leaving Joseph to explain matters, I ran to the children's room: their door was ajar, I saw they had never lain down, though it was past midnight; but they were calmer, and did not need me to console them. The little souls were comforting each other with better thoughts than I could have hit on: no parson in the world ever pictured heaven so beautifully as they did, in their innocent talk; and, while I sobbed and listened, I could not help wishing we were all there safe together.

Mr Hindley came home to the funeral; and—a thing that amazed us, and set the neighbours gossiping right and left—he brought a wife with him. What she was, and where she was born, he never informed us: probably, she had neither money nor name to recommend her, or he would scarcely have kept the union from his father.

She was not one that would have disturbed the house much on her own account. Every object she saw, the moment she crossed the threshold, appeared to delight her, and every circumstance that took place about her: except the preparing for the burial, and the presence of the mourners. I thought she was half silly, from her behaviour while that went on: she ran into her chamber, and made me come with her, though I should have been dressing the children; and there she sat shivering and clasping her hands, and asking repeatedly—"Are they gone yet?" Then she began describing with hysterical emotion the effect it produced on her to see black; and started, and trembled, and, at last, fell a-weeping—and when I asked what was the matter? answered, she didn't know; but she felt so afraid of dying! I imagined her as little likely to die as myself. She was rather thin, but young, and fresh complexioned, and her eyes sparkled as bright as diamonds. I did remark, to be sure, that mounting the stairs made her breathe very quick; that the least sudden noise set her all in a quiver, and that she coughed troublesomely sometimes: but I knew nothing of what these symptoms portended, and had no impulse to sympathize with her. We don't in general take to foreigners here, Mr Lockwood, unless they take to us first.

Young Earnshaw was altered considerably in the three years of his absence. He had grown sparer, and lost his colour, and spoke and dressed quite differently; and, on the very day of his return, he told Joseph and me we must thenceforth quarter ourselves in the back-kitchen, and leave the house for him. Indeed, he would have carpeted and papered a small spare room for a parlour; but his wife expressed such pleasure at the white floor and huge glowing fire-place, at the pewter dishes and delf-case, and dog-kennel, and the wide space there was to move about in where they usually sat, that he thought it unnecessary to her comfort, and so dropped the intention.

She expressed pleasure, too, at finding a sister among her new acquaintance; and she prattled to Catherine, and kissed her, and ran about with her, and gave her quantities of presents, at the beginning. Her affection tired very soon, however, and when she grew peevish,

Hindley became tyrannical. A few words from her, evincing a dislike to Heathcliff, were enough to rouse in him all his old hatred of the boy. He drove him from their company to the servants, deprived him of the instructions of the curate, and insisted that he should labour out of doors instead; compelling him to do so as hard as any other lad on the farm.

Heathcliff bore his degradation pretty well at first, because Cathy taught him what she learnt, and worked or played with him in the fields. They both promised fair to grow up as rude as savages; the young master being entirely negligent how they behaved, and what they did, so they kept clear of him. He would not even have seen after their going to church on Sundays, only Joseph and the curate reprimanded his carelessness when they absented themselves; and that reminded him to order Heathcliff a flogging, and Catherine a fast from dinner or supper. But it was one of their chief amusements to run away to the moors in the morning and remain there all day, and the after punishment grew a mere thing to laugh at. The curate might set as many chapters as he pleased for Catherine to get by heart, and Joseph might thrash Heathcliff till his arm ached; they forgot everything the minute they were together again: at least the minute they had contrived some naughty plan of revenge; and many a time I've cried to myself to watch them growing more reckless daily, and I not daring to speak a syllable for fear of losing the small power I still retained over the unfriended creatures. One Sunday evening, it chanced that they were banished from the sitting-room for making a noise, or a light offence of the kind; and when I went to call them to supper, I could discover them nowhere. We searched the house, above and below, and the yard and stables; they were invisible: and, at last, Hindley in a passion told us to bolt the doors, and swore nobody should let them in that night. The household went to bed; and I, too anxious to lie down,

opened my lattice and put my head out to hearken,
though it rained: determined to admit them in spite of
the prohibition, should they return. In a while, I distinguished steps coming up the road, and the light of
a lantern glimmered through the gate. I threw a shawl
over my head and ran to prevent them from waking
Mr Earnshaw by knocking. There was Heathcliff, by
himself: it gave me a start to see him alone.

"Where is Miss Catherine?" I cried hurriedly. "No
accident, I hope?" "At Thrushcross Grange," he
answered; "and I would have been there too, but they
had not the manners to ask me to stay." "Well, you will
catch it!" I said: "you'll never be content till you're
sent about your business. What in the world led you
wandering to Thrushcross Grange?" "Let me get off
my wet clothes, and I'll tell you all about it, Nelly," he
replied. I bid him beware of rousing the master, and
while he undressed and I waited to put out the candle,
he continued—"Cathy and I escaped from the wash-
house to have a ramble at liberty, and getting a glimpse
of the Grange lights, we thought we would just go and
see whether the Lintons passed their Sunday evenings
standing shivering in corners, while their father and
mother sat eating and drinking, and singing and laughing, and burning their eyes out before the fire. Do you
think they do? Or reading sermons, and being catechized
by their man-servant, and set to learn a column of
Scripture names, if they don't answer properly?"
"Probably not," I responded. "They are good children,
no doubt, and don't deserve the treatment you receive,
for your bad conduct." "Don't cant, Nelly," he said:
"nonsense! We ran from the top of the Heights to the
park, without stopping—Catherine completely beaten
in the race, because she was barefoot. You'll have to
seek for her shoes in the bog to-morrow. We crept
through a broken hedge, groped our way up the path,
and planted ourselves on a flower-plot under the drawing-

room window. The light came from thence; they had
not put up the shutters, and the curtains were only half
closed. Both of us were able to look in by standing on
the basement, and clinging to the ledge, and we saw—ah!
it was beautiful—a splendid place carpeted with crimson,
and crimson-covered chairs and tables, and a pure white
ceiling bordered by gold, a shower of glass-drops hanging
in silver chains from the centre, and shimmering with
little soft tapers. Old Mr and Mrs Linton were not there;
Edgar and his sister had it entirely to themselves.
Shouldn't they have been happy? We should have
thought ourselves in heaven! And now, guess what your
good children were doing? Isabella—I believe she is
eleven, a year younger than Cathy—lay screaming at
the farther end of the room, shrieking as if witches were
running red-hot needles into her. Edgar stood on the
hearth weeping silently, and in the middle of the table
sat a little dog, shaking its paw and yelping; which, from
their mutual accusations, we understood they had nearly
pulled in two between them. The idiots! That was their
pleasure! to quarrel who should hold a heap of warm
hair, and each begin to cry because both, after struggling
to get it, refused to take it. We laughed outright at the
petted things; we did despise them! When would you
catch me wishing to have what Catherine wanted? or
find us by ourselves, seeking entertainment in yelling,
and sobbing, and rolling on the ground, divided by the
whole room? I'd not exchange, for a thousand lives,
my condition here, for Edgar Linton's at Thrushcross
Grange—not if I might have the privilege of flinging
Joseph off the highest gable, and painting the house-
front with Hindley's blood!"

"Hush, hush!" I interrupted. "Still you have not
told me, Heathcliff, how Catherine is left behind?"

"I told you we laughed," he answered. "The Lintons
heard us, and with one accord they shot like arrows to
the door; there was silence, and then a cry, 'Oh, mamma,
mamma! Oh, papa! Oh, mamma, come here. Oh,

papa, oh!' They really did howl out something in that
way. We made frightful noises to terrify them still more,
and then we dropped off the ledge, because somebody
was drawing the bars, and we felt we had better flee.
I had Cathy by the hand, and was urging her on, when
all at once she fell down. 'Run, Heathcliff, run!' she
whispered. 'They have let the bull-dog loose, and he
holds me!' The devil had seized her ankle, Nelly: I heard
his abominable snorting. She did not yell out—no! she
would have scorned to do it, if she had been spitted on
the horns of a mad cow. I did, though: I vociferated
curses enough to annihilate any fiend in Christendom;
and I got a stone and thrust it between his jaws, and
tried with all my might to cram it down his throat.
A beast of a servant came up with a lantern, at last,
shouting—'Keep fast, Skulker, keep fast!' He changed
his note, however, when he saw Skulker's game. The dog
was throttled off; his huge, purple tongue hanging half
a foot out of his mouth, and his pendent lips streaming
with bloody slaver. The man took Cathy up; she was
sick: not from fear, I'm certain, but from pain. He
carried her in; I followed, grumbling execrations and
vengeance. 'What prey, Robert?' hallooed Linton from
the entrance. 'Skulker has caught a little girl, sir,' he
replied; 'and there's a lad here,' he added, making a
clutch at me, 'who looks an out-and-outer! Very like,
the robbers were for putting them through the window
to open the doors to the gang after all were asleep, that
they might murder us at their ease. Hold your tongue,
you foul-mouthed thief, you! you shall go to the gallows
for this. Mr Linton, sir, don't lay by your gun.' 'No, no,
Robert,' said the old fool. 'The rascals knew that yesterday was my rent-day: they thought to have me cleverly.
Come in; I'll furnish them a reception. There, John,
fasten the chain. Give Skulker some water, Jenny. To
beard a magistrate in his stronghold, and on the Sabbath,
too! Where will their insolence stop? Oh, my dear Mary,
look here! Don't be afraid, it is but a boy—yet the

villain scowls so plainly in his face; would it not be a kindness to the country to hang him at once, before he shows his nature in acts as well as features?' He pulled me under the chandelier, and Mrs Linton placed her spectacles on her nose and raised her hands in horror. The cowardly children crept nearer, also, Isabella lisping—'Frightful thing! Put him in the cellar, papa. He's exactly like the son of the fortune-teller, that stole my tame pheasant. Isn't he, Edgar?'

"While they examined me, Cathy came round; she heard the last speech, and laughed. Edgar Linton, after an inquisitive stare, collected sufficient wit to recognize her. They see us at church, you know, though we seldom meet them elsewhere. 'That's Miss Earnshaw!' he whispered to his mother, 'and look how Skulker has bitten her—how her foot bleeds!'

"'Miss Earnshaw? Nonsense!' cried the dame; 'Miss Earnshaw scouring the country with a gipsy! And yet, my dear, the child is in mourning—surely it is—and she may be lamed for life!'

"'What culpable carelessness in her brother!' exclaimed Mr Linton, turning from me to Catherine. 'I've understood from Shielders'" (that was the curate, sir) "'that he lets her grow up in absolute heathenism. But who is this? Where did she pick up this companion? Oho! I declare he is that strange acquisition my late neighbour made, in his journey to Liverpool—a little Lascar, or an American or Spanish castaway.'

"'A wicked boy, at all events,' remarked the old lady, 'and quite unfit for a decent house! Did you notice his language, Linton? I'm shocked that my children should have heard it.'

"I recommenced cursing—don't be angry, Nelly—and so Robert was ordered to take me off. I refused to go without Cathy; he dragged me into the garden, pushed the lantern into my hand, assured me that Mr Earnshaw should be informed of my behaviour, and, bidding me march directly, secured the door again. The curtains were still looped up at one corner, and I resumed my station as spy; because, if Catherine had wished to return, I intended shattering their great glass panes to a million of fragments, unless they let her out. She sat on the sofa quietly. Mrs Linton took off the grey cloak of the dairy-maid which we had borrowed for our excursion, shaking her head and expostulating with her, I suppose: she was a young lady, and they made a distinction between her treatment and mine. Then the woman-servant brought a basin of warm water, and washed her feet; and Mr Linton mixed a tumbler of negus, and Isabella emptied a plateful of cakes into her lap, and Edgar stood gaping at a distance. Afterwards, they dried and combed her beautiful hair, and gave her a pair of enormous slippers, and wheeled her to the fire; and I left her, as merry as she could be, dividing her food between the little dog and Skulker, whose nose she pinched as he ate; and kindling a spark of spirit in the vacant blue eyes of the Lintons—a dim reflection from her own enchanting face. I saw they were full of stupid admiration; she is so immeasurably superior to them— to everybody on earth, is she not, Nelly?"

"There will more come of this business than you reckon on," I answered, covering him up and extinguishing the light. "You are incurable, Heathcliff; and Mr Hindley will have to proceed to extremities, see if he won't." My words came truer than I desired. The luckless adventure made Earnshaw furious. And then Mr Linton, to mend matters, paid us a visit himself on the morrow; and read the young master such a lecture on the road he guided his family, that he was stirred to look about him in earnest. Heathcliff received no flogging, but he was told that the first word he spoke to Miss Catherine should ensure a dismissal; and Mrs Earnshaw undertook to keep her sister-in-law in due restraint when she returned home; employing art, not force: with force she would have found it impossible.

For EU product safety concerns, contact us at Calle de José Abascal, 56–1°, 28003 Madrid, Spain or eugpsr@cambridge.org.

www.ingramcontent.com/pod-product-compliance
Ingram Content Group UK Ltd.
Pitfield, Milton Keynes, MK11 3LW, UK
UKHW012331130625
459647UK00009B/213